The Bright Side of Blue

"My dear friend, Becky Drace, has been on a journey. It's a journey of hills and valleys, quiet streams, rushing rivers, and even rough mountains. However, I suspect we have all been on similar journeys at some time… because this journey is called Life. At times, I'm sure she was tempted to just sit in the grass, looking up at the next mountain or rushing stream, and say to herself, 'This is enough… I can't.' But, I am very grateful she listened to her husband, Jerry, and to the Holy Spirit, and decided to keep on going—and now she shares her heart and her journey with us. What an inspiration it is!"

-GiGi Graham Tchividjian
Daughter of Dr. Billy Graham, Author of
A Quiet Knowing, Weatherproof Your Heart, Prodigals and Those Who Love Them
(co-authored with Ruth Bell Graham), and other titles

"Language is the key to growth and longevity. Jesus is the language of God. Becky Drace has given language to the inevitable spiral that she identifies as despair, discouragement, despondency, and depression. Being a follower of Jesus requires that we recognize that He, too, experienced this spiral. His followers will for certain deal with what Becky calls bright-blue and dark-blue days.

Becky has given us the words that shed light upon our path and serve as instructional guides for what St. John of the Cross labeled as the 'dark night of the soul.' She brings her message from personal experience and the experience of many others. *The Bright Side of Blue* is bound to help many who are on the journey."

-Fr. George Ivey
Canon Missioner, Anglican Diocese of the South

"Becky Drace's lifetime of ministry with families has given her wisdom to reflect on God's faithfulness, whether the sky is bright blue or as dark as midnight. She tells her own story alongside those of others who have experienced the myriad of ways that life experiences knock us around, and she relies on these testimonies and on the Scriptures to offer inspiring words of encouragement to readers. "

-Mary Ann Poe, BA, MSSW, M.Div.
Director of the Center for Just and Caring Communities in Jackson, TN;
Former Dean of the Social Work Department at Union University

"It is a pleasure for me to recommend and commend Becky Drace's new book, *The Bright Side of Blue*. As a pastor and marriage and family therapist for over fifty years, I've walked with many people through dark and deep valleys. I believe Becky's approach of encouragement, introspection, and Scripture will be a help to many people.

Life can be beautiful, sunny, energetic, and filled with all the good things that we desire. But in a flash, that beautiful day can be shattered by bad news or death or illness or loss. We all experience these things. *The Bright Side of Blue* touches the heart of these emotions.

The thing I loved, loved, loved about this book is that it is happy! Becky did an excellent job of blending the real with the hope. The book just fills your soul with joy, no matter what you are going through. I loved her honest testimony of her own life, but I loved the stories from the other people as well. And her bringing the story of Hannah into the picture just seemed to round out the emotions. The questions at the end of the chapters will be great guides for discussion in groups.

Thank you, Becky, for being so open about your struggles and incorporating the struggles of others. But, most of all, thank you for being so encouraging and showing that, through Jesus, there is help and hope and joy."

-Dr. Paul Barkley, EdD
Licensed Marriage and Family Therapist (LMFT)
and Licensed Professional Counselor
with Mental Health Provider Status (LPC/MHPS)

"Becky has written her journey through 'blue' in a personal, easy-to-read, and identifiable style. Since most of us walk through seasons of joy and seasons of difficulty, we find ourselves almost speaking aloud as we read, saying, 'That's me,' or, 'I understand.' We often hear the cliches of 'Look on the bright side,' or, 'Things will get better tomorrow.' Walking through 'dark blue' does not respond to cliches. Although believers know the true light of God's promises, life's circumstances can often turn them dark, as Becky explains. Thank you, Becky, for sharing your journey and recovery with us."

-Ouida Phillips
Wife of Dr. Tom Phillips,
Vice President of the Billy Graham Evangelistic Association

The
BRIGHT
SIDE of
BLUE

Finding Hope in the
Dark Places of Life

BECKY DRACE

NASHVILLE

NEW YORK • LONDON • MELBOURNE • VANCOUVER

The Bright Side of Blue

Finding Hope in the Dark Places of Life

Published in New York, New York, by Morgan James Publishing. Morgan James is a trademark of Morgan James, LLC. www.MorganJamesPublishing.com

Proudly distributed by Publishers Group West®

Scripture quotations used in this book are from The New International Version Disciple's Study Bible, copyright © 1988 by Holman Bible Publishers. Used by permission. All rights reserved.

Morgan James BOGO™

A **FREE** ebook edition is available for you or a friend with the purchase of this print book.

_____

CLEARLY SIGN YOUR NAME ABOVE

Instructions to claim your free ebook edition:
1. Visit MorganJamesBOGO.com
2. Sign your name CLEARLY in the space above
3. Complete the form and submit a photo of this entire page
4. You or your friend can download the ebook to your preferred device

ISBN 9781636985220 paperback
ISBN 9781636985237 ebook
Library of Congress Control Number: 2024940159

Cover & Interior Design by:
Christopher Kirk
www.GFSstudio.com

Morgan James PUBLISHING Builds with... Habitat for Humanity Peninsula and Greater Williamsburg

Morgan James is a proud partner of Habitat for Humanity Peninsula and Greater Williamsburg. Partners in building since 2006.

Get involved today! Visit: www.morgan-james-publishing.com/giving-back

I dedicate this book to my husband, Dr. Jerry L. Drace, and to our children, Drew and Becca, their spouses, Joshua and Lisa, and our grandchildren, Nick, Noah, Isa, Levi, and Hannah …

… and to any person who has ever had a bright-blue peak of life change to a dark-blue valley of discouragement. There is hope for you, my friend.

Table of Contents

Foreword by Mike Huckabee. xi
Introduction 1

1.   The Beginning of Blue 2
2.   What's the Difference?. 4
3.   Losing Focus 7
4.   Keep on Going 14
5.   A Peace That Passes. 19
6.   When the Path Is Dark Blue 24
7.   Trusting through Betrayal. 29
8.   The Blue of Pain and Hurt 33
9.   Behind the Scenes. 38
10.   The Blue of Broken Pieces 43
11.   The Dark Blue of the Wilderness .48
12.   Prayers through the Dark Blue 52
13.   Rolling On—I'm Still Here 56
14.   Flow with the Go. 60
15.   Moving from Dark to Light 63
16.   Attitude Is Everything 67
17.   The Progression of Blue 69
18.   My Personal Story Continues. 73
19.   Lessons Learned along the Path. .79
20.   Where to Find What You Need. 86
21.   The Story of Hannah 88

22.   The Spiral Begins 91
23.   Marriage Madness..............................95
24.   Worship Worries 97
25.   À Sensitive Spouse 100
26.   Blue Brightens 103
27.   Bright Blue Returns............................107
28.   The Bright Side of Blue Continues 109

Appendix: Steps to the Bright-Blue Place........................111
Acknowledgments 113
About the Author 115

Foreword

I've known Becky Drace and her husband Jerry for forty years. They have been faithful in ministry to thousands of people in their evangelistic work and pastoral ministry. They have been steadfast and faithful in their devotion to each other and to the Lord and His work.

But, like all believers, that doesn't mean that every day is lived on the mountaintop. Some days are endured from the lowest of the valleys in our pilgrimage to follow Christ. Becky tells of her own journey, but the true brilliance of the book is that she gives voice to many other believers who anonymously share their own journey through the best and worst of times.

We are reminded that being a believer doesn't exempt us from experiencing crises of health, financial ruin, infidelity of a deeply trusted marriage partner, or the betrayal of those believed to be close friends—even from church. It's not that we will experience these harsh chapters, but how we will respond to them that determines if our "walk through the valley of the shadow of death" takes us to encouragement or despair.

There is a very good likelihood that you will recognize your own journey in the stories of these folks who bare their souls to honestly disclose pain they weren't expecting and didn't think they could endure. Ultimately, this is not a book that will allow you to wallow in your misery but will help you to understand that there is NO circumstance so dire and to be beyond the grace and goodness of God.

You will love the study questions at the end of each chapter, which are helpful in putting together the truth learned from our pain or to use in a group study. However you use the book and its message, it will be a blessing and a guide toward a life encouraged!

-Mike Huckabee
44th Governor of the State of Arkansas,
2008 and 2016 Presidential Candidate,
Ordained Southern Baptist Pastor,
Political Commentator, Host of *Huckabee* on TBN

Introduction

I t's interesting how a perfectly beautiful, bright-blue day can grow darker when some unexpected challenge arises. Despair, discouragement, or depression can enter slowly or suddenly. In much the same way, everybody will experience blue periods along the journey of life.

I have spent my entire married life engaged with my husband, Jerry, in full-time evangelistic ministry. Our home was my mission outpost. I felt fulfilled and content. I loved that. Then life changed. Our daughter, Becca, joined her brother, Drew, in college and my nest emptied out. I lost my sense of purpose and direction. That began my first real plunge into a dark-blue place.

The second major event was a diagnosis of "cancer" on December 27, 2021. The test results indicated Stage 1—Triple Positive Breast Cancer. I began chemotherapy treatment on January 14, 2022.

Since chemo therapy weakens your entire system, I had to be extra careful of "viruses" that might be floating around. This created new challenges. I had to stay clear of what I love the most: people. I had to lean more on Jerry our family and our close friends. I had to find strength.

This book shares my journey.

1

The Beginning of Blue

S ince I am normally a bright, sunny person, being faced with an empty nest and then later the diagnosis of "cancer" hit me hard. I had difficulty processing the immediate facts and then I had multiple questions that followed.

The shock of cancer resulted in an emotional shift into the second period of deep dark "blueness." I hadn't experienced this level of dark blue in a very long time. I had to process what was happening. Jerry encouraged me to write about my experiences, so I began to journal about how my life events were causing abrupt changes to everything I once considered normal. Writing down my thoughts led me into a new area I had not considered. I had an epiphany one day during my quiet time!

It was this: Not everyone looks at their empty nest in the same way as I did. Some parents are glad when their kids leave home. Also, not everyone goes through cancer but every person has challenges that can abruptly shake their world. This led me to explore how people cope and move through different types of life experiences.

Along the path of my life journey, I have met hundreds of people who have shared with me their stories, so I began to think outside of my personal box. I began to ask a series of questions to some of the people I had met: *How have you coped? How would you encourage others?*

The trajectory of my book shifted from my life challenge to others' experiences.

I discovered a wide array of areas where both men and women face a myriad of changing emotions due to some life event. Every individual I interviewed revealed periods of confusion, sadness, and, yes, even depression. All of the stories revealed deeply personal experiences with similar common themes that helped them navigate their challenges. Two of these were **FAITH** and **HOPE**.

Faith carries when all hope seems lost. Faith gives strength and courage to take one day at a time and often even one step at a time. The most desperate place for any person is to lose all hope and to have their faith shaken.

My story begins just like every other story. I was faced with facts and feelings I had never before experienced. I was confused, scared, frustrated, fretful, and angry. I shifted from the bright blue of my ordinary life into a shadowy time of clouded blueness. Some days seemed overwhelming while others were easier. I had to discover how to navigate the new challenges and where to find the courage and strength to forge through.

Therefore, I begin my book with a portion of my walk into the dark blue. I will then share various stories of what some other individuals have faced and how they managed to return from a shifting, dark-blue experience back to a brighter, more positive, place in life.

The question that almost consumed me was, "Becky, are you in despair and despondency, or have you moved into a state of depression?" Some days it was blurry because emotions are tricky.

Men and women process life through different filters. As we all go through these emotional stages where life is interrupted, each person must find their personal way to handle what life has thrown their way. For me, it was a test of my faith and resilience. Without a personal relationship with God through His Son, Jesus, I could not have written a positive ending to my story.

There are eleven stories included in my book that reveal interesting and, I pray, inspirational perspectives to encourage you along the paths of your life. These stories are some of the more common areas of life's challenges.

At the end of each story, you will find an opportunity for personal reflection. I conclude the book with the rest of my story and then with a story of a person from the Bible: Hannah. The story of Hannah is an example of the impact of depression on life. It is a powerful picture of how a person can spiral back from a deep, dark-blue place to a bright-blue place in life. My prayer AS you complete this book is that the life of Hannah will inspire and encourage you along your path of life.

Blessings as you read.

2

What's the Difference?

I s there a difference between despair, discouragement, despondency, and depression? Yes!

Despair may be a fleeting thought or situation. It can be dispelled by looking for ways to be positive instead of dwelling on the negatives. *Discouragement* comes to everyone at some point in life. Usually this is quickly overridden by refocusing. *Despondency* may stay a little while. It might come along because of any new life challenge that is out of the ordinary. It could be because of a situation at work, a change of jobs, relocation or a relationship challenge. It might take a little time to work through what is going on.

Sometimes the slightest change in routine can swing a person into despair, discouragement, or despondency. For most people, this is temporary. However, the deepest place of blue is *depression.* The longer a person stays in a state of despair, discouragement, or despondency the more probable it may spiral deeper into this state.

How many people do you know who have dealt with depression or are currently going through a personal emotional or mental crisis? How pervasive is depression? No one is immune to the possibility of becoming consumed by an event in life.

Research indicates that, in the past three years, depression has become a national and international issue. It is becoming one of the most nagging medical problems of our culture. It affects all ages, genders, races, and economic backgrounds.

There is no person who is exempt from the possibility of riding the emotional rollercoaster of depression. The American Psychological Association reports the need for psychological services is at an all-time high. Their report reveals:

- 1 in 5 children experience mental anguish.
- In 2020, 72% of parents said the pandemic had an impact on their child's mental health.
- A national survey of 3,300 high school students found close to 1 in 3 felt unhappy or depressed more than usual.
- 20% of adolescent girls and 6.8 % of adolescent boys experience depression.
- 4.1 million adolescents have experienced at least one depressive episode since 2021.
- 3.1 million children ages 12 to 17 may have serious depression issues.
- 22.5% of women and 21% of men report experiencing depression.
- Overall research indicates 1 in 10 Americans experience depression.

Depression is not a respecter of age, as research reveals. Children may not understand why they are sad or know how to cope with the changes in their emotions. Teenagers may not be able to think through what is going on in their lives and may become withdrawn (more than usual).

Some of the data suggests maturity and growth, changes in family structure, challenges of school life, lack of parental attention, or simply a natural tendency to keep to themselves may be contributing factors to depression in children and teens.

We are told by media and selected professionals just to work hard at our job or fill our time with whatever we choose. "Just listen and do what we say and your depression will go away eventually." We are also told that medication is an answer. There are many opinions as to the cause of depression and how to overcome its results.

Depression can have an effect on everyone in the home. When parents become overwhelmed, the children may sense unrest without ever hearing a word spoken. They may pick up on the emotional status of Dad or Mom. On the other hand, parents may not be aware that a child is struggling.

We may receive the impression that being depressed is a weakness. It is not! It is a formidable foe that need not become an overwhelming, all-consuming fire.

It is vital to the individual, family, and society as a whole that we address emotional and mental issues. There are multiple ways to encourage those who are struggling. Help is available!

Not every event of life will bring on an emotional upset. Most people can maneuver through life by taking each day as it comes and can control emotions by using whatever coping mechanism they have in place. But what happens when life is interrupted by some unexpected event? This may shift what started out to be a regular, bright-blue day into a dark-blue place filled with swirling emotions.

One person told me that even though she was normally a bright, sunny person most of the time, the events of her life had beaten her into a place of darkness. There were times I felt that way, too.

> **1 Peter 5:7**
> *"Cast all your anxieties on Him because He cares for you."*

Questions for you to consider:

1. Would you consider yourself bright and sunny or more introspective? Why?
2. What would be one mountain peak (a high) that you have experienced in life?
3. What would be one valley (a low) that you have walked through?
4. Have you ever shifted from a normal place of bright blue into a dark-blue place?
5. How did you handle the situation?

3

Losing Focus

My story begins with the empty nest but then, a few years later, cancer entered my world. It took me a few weeks to work my way mentally and emotionally through the harsh fact that I had cancer. I threw all the questions I could think of out to God. Every question was answered in the same way.

"Becky, Just take one day at a time. Seek Me and I will guide you every step of the way, every day."

> ### Matthew 6:33–34
> "Seek first the Kingdom of God and His righteousness and all these things will be added unto you. Do not worry about tomorrow for tomorrow will worry about itself. Each day has enough trouble of its own."

Many people have difficulty moving from one life stage to another. It seems that women have more trouble in this area than men. Some just can't seem to stay focused and positive.

Our remedy, whenever a disruption occurred in our home, was to talk it out and pray it through, sometimes with tears and a bit of gritted teeth. No matter who was out of sorts or sad, our family always managed to just remember that "this will pass."

Our children often labeled days in colors. Red days were "really happy days." Yellow days were sunny with nothing scheduled except play. Green days were "yard work days." Gray days were the dead-of-winter days when it was cold and overcast. Then there were those "blue" days. It may have begun as a bright-blue and cheerful day, then changed with the day speeding out of control into craziness.

On the way home from school one afternoon, our son, Drew, was upset because one of his friends was being bullied. The teachers had ignored what all the students knew. Drew couldn't understand how kids could be so mean. He was angry, frustrated, and sad all at the same time. He was trying to process how he felt. It had definitely turned into a "dark-blue" day.

When our daughter, Becca, had a dark-blue day, everybody knew it. Her body language was transparent. She might cry, frown, grumble, or moan.

It's interesting, the different ways people handle the challenges in life. Some are open and transparent; others are closed and introspective. Jerry just moves through. I tend first to close up then openly blubber!

Although it was usually easy for our family to work through events that disrupted our lives, a couple were very hard for me. Several years ago, I found myself faced with a new situation. I was beginning a spiral into a blue place that I could not control. Have you ever been in this place?

Our daughter, Becca, was packing for college. Our son, Drew, was going through some relationship issues and I sensed that I was beginning to go through "the change." I couldn't sleep at night, which for me is a major problem. I have to have at least seven hours of "good" sleep to function during the day.

With our nest emptying out and my emotions so fragile, I was losing my focus. I began to doubt my ability to be effective in speaking and then lost sight of my personal mission. What once was my passion to minister to women was quickly being diluted by my emotional instability.

I was rapidly spiraling out of control and I was becoming more withdrawn and disagreeable. My husband, Jerry, and our children, didn't want my company, which drove me further into myself.

I tried to talk with some of my older friends to see how they handled "the change." To my dismay, everyone had a different suggestion. I read about herbal treatment, teas, and supplements. I even tried aromatherapy and a massage.

I cried a lot at night into my pillow. I was tired of lying awake at night and listening to Jerry snore. I became jealous of his sleep and the more he tried to comfort me, the more hateful I acted. I would stifle my sobs as best as possible.

Actually, my family did not realize how deeply into despair I had fallen. I knew I was becoming depressed. I was frustrated. I couldn't see how to move forward.

As an educated and trained professional, I knew all the agencies that dealt with depression, but I decided to take a route aside from intervention, using a holistic approach.

Please know it is important to look at personal depression and to seek professional assistance if necessary, but I firmly believe that the best place to begin is in a personal analysis and then a search of Scripture. You just might find this to be the "dot over the I" or the "icing on the cake."

There is absolutely no substitute for the power the Word of God and prayer can have on ANY and ALL situations in life. How can I say this? I have lived by these standards since the age of sixteen.

I became a believer in Jesus at age nine. At age sixteen, I made a monumental decision that changed the direction of my life. I decided to commit 100 percent of my life to follow Christ and decided to claim Scripture. I can look back and see how that commitment to God has moved me back from several dark-blue places of despair to bright-blue places of hope and peace. It has again come to rest in my life.

After several months of being in an emotional pit, I knew I had to do something. I had put aside my Bible (bad choice) because I was angry at my situation.

During our parenting years, I had invested time and energy into our son and daughter and their friends. Our home had been filled with the bright blue of laughter and fun. By being available and investing my time in them, I had learned so much about their lives and the lives of their friends. I considered our home my mission outpost. A bright-blue place.

A darker blue began to creep in. I began to feel that my life of service might, in fact, be over. Have you ever been in that place? I began to be mad at God. I had lots of questions. That's okay. Nowhere in the Bible does it say you can't ask questions. Many of the saints of Scripture went into blue places of despair. Even our Lord, during His travail in the garden just before the cross, had questions for the Father.

As I asked God for answers, He led me to where I needed to go: His Word. The power of God slowly began to restore me. Mind you, slowly!

Then, several years later, another major challenge arose. I was shocked to hear the words "breast cancer." I was overcome with information about options and treatment possibilities. I began to spiral back into a very deep, dark-blue place. So many questions.

During my earlier experience with the empty nest and depression, I had gone to my doctor of many years, Dr. Keith Williams, because I knew I could trust him to help me. Trusted physicians can become a good place to seek answers.

He listened, then leaned back, crossed his legs, and said, "Let's pray first." Then his response was, "I can prescribe medicine but this will only treat your premenopausal symptoms. I think you have become self-consumed with your 'situation.' Your focus is out of whack. There is no medical treatment for that. You have to shift your emphasis from yourself back to others. Let me suggest you seek God!"

That annoyed me. How could this physician know so much about my spiritual condition? God used him to speak to me physically and spiritually. He prayed for me.

I learned from my caring and sensitive doctor that before I needed medical intervention I needed to examine where I had fallen spiritually. A Christian doctor can look beyond the physical issue.

I have fallen from my bright-blue place in life several times since that initial plummet. Life challenges can be hard to handle.

Becca asked me once in a bit of heated discussion, "Mom, does everything have a spiritual basis?"

After thinking for just a moment, I answered, "Well, according to the Bible, yes, it does."

I have found that even though life has many pitfalls where the dark-blue place can become all-consuming, God in His goodness has given us a place to begin recovery.

Having a relationship with Him through His Son, Jesus, is that place. Prayer, God's Word, and reliance on His wisdom is where the bright-blue places of life reside. The dark-blue places come when we lose sight of God's grace and mercy and provision to assist us in life's crises and drama.

As I began the process through cancer, it immediately took me back to a dark-blue place. A place of questioning. *What does this mean? Will I live long? Whom do I go to? What questions do I need to ask? How can God use this in my life? Will He?*

I then said, "Lord, help me!"

From that second, He began to work in me. God reminded me that, years earlier, I received wise counsel from a good doctor.

I asked God to speak to me; I felt a surge of power. I allowed God's Word to filter into my spirit. Over the next bit of time, I found my attitude begin to change. I had become sad, fretful, and brooding. I knew it.

A Bible verse came to mind, Matthew 6:33–34:

> "Seek ye first the Kingdom of God and His righteousness and ALL these things will be added unto you. Therefore do not be anxious for tomorrow for tomorrow will take care of itself. Each day has enough trouble of its own."

To what things was Jesus referring? Simple things. *The birds and flowers do not worry or fret. They are only concerned with accepting the provision and care of God. Then, Becky, you, too, need not be anxious.* That spoke to my heart.

I also added a good dose of thanksgiving. Each time a negative thought crept in, I would make a mental list of the things for which to be grateful. I wrote them down. I still do that today in the middle of cancer treatment.

First Thessalonians 5:18 says: *"In everything give thanks for this is the will of God for you in Christ Jesus."* This verse is miraculous in its ability to change attitudes. The assurance of Scripture can be the beginning of healing.

Focusing on simple things and adding thanksgiving with prayer will aid in the healing process. God's Holy Spirit spoke to me with this counsel: *Becky, as you begin to think clearly, you will be able to return to the bright blue.*

As the emotions settled, the cloud began to lift. I needed a doctor who would treat me physically, emotionally, and spiritually.

Our daughter in love, Lisa, connected me with the Baptist Breast Cancer Center in Memphis. The medical team is amazing and became my place of treatment. My first appointment with the staff confirmed my decision. This was where I needed to be. This was new territory. I had never traveled this way before.

It's interesting that the advice given to me by my doctor years before and at this time was the same. I had to look at myself first before a treatment plan could be prescribed.

I needed to do some self-evaluation. Would I allow this to overwhelm me? Could God use me through this and how? Would I become self-absorbed? Was I willing to do what is necessary to help me recover?

This health crisis could have led me to into a dark-blue place if I became self-absorbed. There isn't a medical treatment for that!

When I thought about what both doctors said, I felt the sting of truth. I realized how easy it is to allow life's situations to control everything—emotions, responses, and reactions. I had to admit I needed an overhaul. I knew exactly what was required for me to navigate this challenge. I went home. I took my Bible and laid my hands on the cover. That was an amazing day for me!

Once I had completed my treatment process, Jerry encouraged me to write my thoughts. Out of this began a project. Not everyone has to deal with cancer. What other areas of life might lead to a shift from that bright-blue place into a dark-blue emotional place? There are so many.

The spiral into "blue" can happen to anyone. Same symptoms. Different situations. Different people. Perhaps different outcomes. What may begin as a "bit of blue" may grow into an overwhelming, dark-blue abyss.

I began to recall stories I had been told of how people have faced crises such as the death of a spouse or child, caring for an invalid relative, grief, or dealing with affairs, divorce, homosexuality, rape, betrayal, loneliness, relocation, and many other issues.

How do people cope when dark blue sets in? I started to ask.

I listened to many stories and learned that it takes courage to maneuver through the maze when life turns dark blue. Some of the stories were heart wrenching but I saw clearly how incredibly resilient people can be.

As my interviews progressed, I explored how people navigate personal, often painful and unique, challenges to their lives. I heard many stories from many angles and with many outcomes. Some of the interviews caused the resurfacing of painful memories long ago locked into their past. Some brought back joy. Each story is different and deeply personal.

The main question throughout this book is, "How do I return to a brighter-blue place from a dark-blue experience?"

It was hard to decide whose stories to include in my book. I chose eleven. As you read each individual story prayerfully, I pray some of their experiences will resonate and speak to you, too.

> **2 Thessalonians 5:16–18**
> *"Rejoice always, pray without ceasing; in everything give thanks; for this is the will of God for you in Christ Jesus."*

Questions for you to consider:

1. How hard is it for you to be thankful when life seems to be falling apart?
2. Make a list of things for which you are thankful. Begin with only five things.
3. Did you know that it is God's will for you to have a grateful spirit in everything? How does that make you feel?
4. God has four areas that are His general will for every person. See if you can find these four verses in the Bible (Hint: feel free to use an online search engine!)
5. God not only has a general will for every person; He also has a specific will designed just for you. Do you think you have found His will for your life? How do you know (or not)?

4

Keep on Going

A bright or light-blue time in life may be disrupted by an unexpected situation, bringing a whirlwind of up-and-down emotions and the need for changes that impact the future. How a person copes with new life experiences depends on the person.

There are always questions. It takes time to think and develop a plan for moving forward.

Multiple questions are asked, like, "Why, God has this happened? What do I do? Where do I go? Should I seek help? Do I retreat into a solitary place or do I share what I am going through with someone? Whom should I talk to? Whom can I trust?"

How do I just keep on going?

> **1 Peter 5:7**
> *"Cast all your anxieties on Him because He cares for you."*

Just Keep on Going—by K

My life has been a series of unusual events as is true with most everyone. At the age of eighty-three, I've lived a long time, seen a lot, and done a lot. I never thought my life story would include so many different events.

Mostly I consider my life in the middle of blue. Not necessarily bright nor dark blue.

There have been some high points and low points, to be sure. One struggle I've had is within myself. I have always wanted to be in control. Pretty much had myself as a priority. Day by day there was no major drama that I thought I couldn't handle. I wanted to do my best and achieve as much as possible. I studied hard and was valedictorian of my class, so I achieved that goal.

My goal was to finish college and begin a career teaching. All was well. Then an unexpected event happened.

During my early years in college, I carpooled with friends back and forth to the university. On one of the trips, I was riding shotgun, in the front seat of my friend's car. I simply asked him what would he do if he thought we were going to have a wreck. I told him I would fall to the floor board. This was before seat belts and airbags. Just after I asked this question, we wrecked. I did immediately fall to the floor board.

I broke both legs in the accident but, because of my quick reaction, I had no internal or head injuries. Even though I would say I wasn't a religious person, I wondered if God had spared me for some reason.

This wasn't the only unexpected accident in my life. I have broken both legs, both arms, and had shoulder surgery. Through all these injuries, I managed using my life's motto: "Just keep on going."

After graduation from college with a degree in education, I began my teaching career. Again I worked hard, studied hard, and achieved my goals. In one of my classes, a girl student caught my eye. After graduation, she took a job in Memphis. I took a teaching position in Missouri. It wasn't long before I decided to ask M to join me. We married and began our family life together. That was in 1964. We were busy with establishing our home and pursuing our careers.

We didn't have any religious affiliation at that time. One day, a couple of ladies from a local church came by and invited us to attend. My wife said, "K, I think we'll go to church." That began a new awareness of who God is and my need to know Him and His Son, Jesus.

Again, as is common for me, I worked hard at my church, taught Sunday School, and was ordained as a deacon. Now in my senior years, I still attend as much as possible in spite of some health issues. The community of faith that I found in church has been a source of encouragement and support all these years.

M and I were blessed with two daughters and three grandchildren. Life was good. We lived on the family farm, which is actually a "century" farm, having been in my family for over a hundred years.

The greatest challenge of my life happened when M became sick with lung and heart disease. This was a dark-blue phase of our lives. We both tried to manage her daily medications. Watching M struggle day by day was hard. After her death in 2001, there were many questions.

Our faith in God is what sustained us and got me through the dark blue of her illness and death. My motto continued to be "Just keep on going."

I taught Life Science for thirty-nine years. I even taught math during one of my teaching experiences. Because of my love for nature I was able to incorporate that with my teaching. Nature is fascinating.

Birds are particularly interesting to me. There are so many different breeds all with different nesting, mating ,and feeding habits. Quite a life study. I collected bird nests and this expanded my classroom experience, resulting in opportunities to speak in many other schools.

I've met many wonderful people who also have a love for "birds." Even now, I am part of a group that meets for special bird events and for meals. This group of friends has filled many hours which otherwise might have been lonely times for me.

Another challenge was a few years ago when I stumbled, fell over a limb in the woods, and broke my ankle and leg. Again, I "just kept on going."

If you ask me how I manage to move from some dark-blue times back into a brighter-blue place, I would respond with several ways:

1. I accept that there are times when the dark blue moves in and how we cope during those times will result in how and if we return to a brighter-blue place in life.
2. I lean heavily on my relationship with God.
3. I receive encouragement from friends, my girls, and my grandchildren.
4. I stay busy.

People who live alone may experience loneliness. The emotion of loneliness may move a person into a darker place of blue. I may live alone, but I'm not lonely. I fill my time with farm duties. I stay active and involved in my community and church and I just "keep on going." I cling to hope that whatever time I have left will be spent enjoying life in the "bright blue."

My final advice for cultivating a brighter-blue life is to be involved in the lives of others. Circle yourself with like-minded friends and love on people.

A verse from the Bible that is one of my favorites is 2 Chronicles 7:13–14:

> "When I shut up the heavens so that there is no rain, or command locusts to devour the land or send a plague among my people, If my people who are called by my name will humble themselves and pray and seek my face and turn from their wicked ways then will I hear from heaven and will forgive their sin and heal their land. Now my eyes will be open and my ears attentive to the prayers offered in this place."

The other verse that means so much to my life journey is John 13:34–35:

> "A new commandment I give you to love one another. As I have loved you, so you must love one another. By this all men will know that you are my disciples, if you have love for one another."

I have had many people in my life to give me love, encouragement, strength, and direction. Influence is important. This began with my grandparents and parents, my wife and her parents. Now this includes our daughters, their families, and other relatives.

Never underestimate the importance of the surrounding support system that is available to provide you with positive input. Teachers, neighbors, church staff, and members all can contribute to helping anyone move beyond the challenges of life that tend to make us spiral into dark-blue places back to the lighter blue.

In my thirty-nine years in education, I e had thousands of students sit under my teaching. Having responsibility for the minds and hearts of students was an additional way to help me "just keep on going."

The main motivation for me is knowing that God cares, listens, and loves me, no matter what comes along. Wherever you are in life, whether young or older, God knows every challenge before it happens. As you seek Him, He will help you to "just keep on going."

> ### 2 Timothy 4:7
> *"I have fought the good fight. I have finished the course; I have kept the faith."*

Questions for you to consider:

1. How do you respond when unexpected events come into your life?
2. How would you encourage someone to keep moving forward, no matter what comes?
3. Does it seem impossible that the Bible offers everything any person needs to help them continue to maintain an active and productive life?

5

A Peace That Passes All ...

The death of a spouse brings on some of the most difficult times with which to cope. The grieving process has many aspects. As a social work major, I studied the multitude of ways people work through grief. It has length and breadth and depth.

Some people grieve but are able to move on day by day. Others rest in grief. The loss is real and the absence sometimes difficult to accept. The hope for a believer is eternal life in heaven.

> ### John 14:27
> "My peace I leave with you. My peace I give to you, not the peace of the world. Do not let your heart be troubled, neither let it be afraid."

A Peace That Passes All—by MP

My life journey began long before 1976, but in that particular year I moved into a new path that altered my journey. I had been married to my precious wife, L, for three years and I knew she loved me. But there was something deeper. I saw in her an astounding love for Jesus Christ. I realized she had something I did not have.

One Tuesday night we had a visitor to our home, Truett Cathy, founder of Chick-fil-A. He came by for a visit from the church. As we talked, I knew I had not had a soul-awakening experience.

Shortly after that Tuesday evening visit, I invited Jesus to come into my life. His presence changed everything! It was truly a different experience than I had ever had before. I didn't realize how much a relationship with Christ will add to life's journey.

Using a Christian term, I had been "justified" (set right with God). I knew that because of my decision to be a follower of Christ, I should live by His example—that is, to be "sanctified" (grow and mature).

Concepts and perspectives of life change when one becomes a believer in Christ. I began to think more about my ideas regarding finances, faith, and family. My thoughts changed. I realized that everything I owned had been given to me by God to use and enjoy. I knew I needed to be responsible with my money. I began to tithe and then as God blessed that act of obedience; I was able to give to other areas, as well. It is amazing what happens when a person decides to trust God in every area of life!

I have three brothers and, because my life changed so much after I met Jesus, I wanted them to also experience Him in a personal way. I sent them Christian literature and when we talked I would end our conversations by telling them of my love for them, and that I was praying for them. Even though they all attended church, I wanted to be sure they understood how a personal relationship with Christ is more than church attendance.

My new relationship with Christ also affected my relationship with my wife; she and I now shared a mutual relationship that added a deeper love to our marriage. We had both been married before and she had a son. He also had been married before, but during his second marriage, he felt a calling to enter ministry. Now he is not only a husband and father of seven children, but a pastor.

My wife was instrumental in influencing our grandchildren. They all are believers in Christ partly because of how she shared her love for Jesus and them. It's amazing how the love of Christ can spread throughout a family.

My wife was a living breathing totally absorbed believer in Christ. In her career as a representative for several cosmetic companies, in our neighborhood, and in our church, she lived out what we both believed. Jesus' peace passes all understanding and living for Him makes all the difference in everything.

Health issues had been part of my wife's life from the beginning of our marriage. Even though she had lived with these health issues, they did not cause her to waver. She was always filled with joy and used every opportunity to tell people of Jesus' love and care. Even in the hospital she did not stop telling people about Jesus.

Over the years, her health issues worsened. Our local doctor told us they could do nothing more for her and referred her to Mayo Clinic in Minnesota. Eventually Mayo opened in our city. This made it easier to get her to appointments and receive care and treatment.

We have always prayed for others. We know the power of prayer. We had people praying for her and know these prayers brought her courage and strength. God honored the prayers on her behalf and her condition stabilized for a season.

She was able to make a ten-day trip to Israel in 2016, where she had a marvelous time. However, within a few weeks after her return, she developed some cognition problems that resulted in a two-week hospital stay.

I stayed with her 24/7 as I would not leave her alone. We committed to each other when we married to be with each other no matter what might come our way. I wanted her to know that she could always depend on me to be by her side. Love brings two people together to marry but commitment is the glue that will keep a marriage solid.

During the hospital stay, I sensed that things just weren't right. The doctor ordered a brain scan for the next day and we prayed that night that nothing would be found. Lo and behold, the result was they found nothing of concern at that time! Our prayers again were answered. We were released knowing that God's grace was sufficient and we had a peace that was passing all understanding.

Over the next bit of time there were more cognition events that were also short-lived. We felt God's grace. His timing is always perfect whether in health or sickness.

In May 2019, I awoke to find my wife lying on the hall floor, unconscious. Rescue took her to the closest hospital, not Mayo, where she was diagnosed with bleeding on the brain. From May 2019 until February 2020 we were in the hospital, rehab, skilled nursing care, or nursing home. Again, I stayed with her throughout all of her care.

As we bless God, He blesses us and we saw Him working all along the way. Even though the doctors told us she probably would not be able to return home, we were released a couple of weeks before the pandemic hit. This was another miracle from God.

We continued to trust in the Lord each day and we moved back from these cloudy, dark-blue events into a brighter, more normal life. During the pandemic, we could watch sermons on tv since we could not attend church because of her health.

Last year (2022), L was again admitted to the hospital for a GI infection. During that stay, she had three mini strokes, which sent her to rehab. We were released but a few months later I again awoke to find her on the kitchen floor, semiconscious. We were admitted to Mayo where the doctors said they almost lost her. She was in ICU for several days.

She was in horrible pain and suffered with anxiety attacks. Mayo sent in eight to ten doctors to assess her situation. Unlike my sweet wife, she was screaming at everyone due to the pain. Two of our goddaughters observed that she was exhibiting symptoms of dementia. They had seen this in their mother.

A doctor called me into the hall way and said the hospital could no longer manage her pain and she needed hospice care. Sadly, that seemed to be the best plan. After six days in hospice care, L went home to her final resting place, Heaven, with the Lord. It was 12:30 a.m. when the attending nurse woke me to say that she had passed. I got into bed with her and just held her for the next four hours.

No more pain or suffering. She is seeing Jesus and is praising Him. God's grace and mercy put an end to her physical suffering and His mercy and grace give me peace. A Bible verse that sustains me is Philippians 4:7: *"And the peace of God which passes all understanding shall guard you hearts and your minds in Christ Jesus."* No matter how difficult the challenge, I have found that the only way to return from any dark-blue place into a brighter place in life is to simply trust Jesus.

> **1 Corinthians 15:54**
>
> *"But when this perishable has put on the imperishable, and this mortal has put on immortality, then will come about the saying that is written 'Death is swallowed up in victory.'"*

Questions for you to consider:

1. If you have had responsibility for the long-term care of a loved one, how did you take care of your personal needs? How did others help to care for you?

2. What would be your counsel if asked how to make difficult decisions in the care of a loved one?

3. What place does prayer have in making decisions regarding life and death?

4. How important is your relationship with God in your decision-making process?

6

When the Path Is Dark Blue

L ooking backward often brings clarity to what is going on in the present. Each event in life has a tendency to change the trajectory of the future. An accident, illness, or some other situation may halt the ability to perform normal and expected daily activities. It is hard to walk through the darkness without a light to guide the way.

2 Samuel 22:29
"For Thou art my lamp, O Lord, and the Lord illuminates my darkness."

When the Path is Dark Blue — by B

The year was 1998. At thirty-seven years old, I was living well, happy, and working in my dream job as a paramedic and teaching EMS classes part time. One weekend, my husband, brother, and his wife decided to take a trip to Boston— a quick trip to enjoy some time off. This began a dark-blue path for me.

We were driving a rental car from the airport when all of a sudden we were hit hard from behind, a hit-and-run accident. We all seemed fine with no detectable injuries.

Fast forward to 2004. I awoke with numbness in my shoulder, arm, and two fingers. I went to a chiropractor and x-rays confirmed severe whiplash with a herniated disc in my neck. Then I remembered the wreck. After three treatments, I became numb from my waist down to my feet, which frightened me. The doctor was certain this would go away but it did not.

I went to a neurologist, hoping to get answers. After an MRI, the doctor ordered emergency surgery to my neck. He said that without surgery, I would be paralyzed. I was in shock and speechless. While in the pre-op area, I felt alone and scared.

Dark blue can permeate any place at any time when life throws in something unexpected. I ended up having three neck surgeries and, as a result, there was no paralysis. I can function pretty normally, except not in the EMS field. The dark-blue path came as a result of the accident.

The lighter blue place began to return as I settled into my new life. I became a homemaker and I enjoyed that. I was also trying to adjust to the lingering numbness as best as I could. My way back out of the dark blue into the lighter blue was due to being thankful to God. Each day, I thanked Him for bringing me through this with no other issues.

Then another situation emerged. I again found myself moving into the dark blue and this time it struck even harder. I noticed on the Friday of Memorial Day weekend that I was having a ringing in my ears. On Saturday, my husband and I went for my Ham Radio test. We were walking through hall of exhibits when a microphone made a very high shrill noise and my ears immediately reacted. By bedtime, the ringing had gone down but in the middle of the night I was awakened to a blaring in my ears so loud that I thought I was going to lose my mind.

After a trip to the clinic, the diagnosis was sinusitis. The shot they gave me didn't make the noise go away. Back to the ENT I went. The result was that I would just have to learn to live with the ringing.

The dark blue of a hopeless diagnosis consumed me and I completely fell apart. I cried and screamed at God. I begged God to please heal me. *How can I go on with this constant screeching in my ears and head? Why, since I am so young and have the rest of my life ahead?* This was the darkest blue day of my life.

The tinnitus is affected by different levels of noise. There is always a low noise like crickets chirping. Some days the chirping is low, other days high. I did not want to accept that I would have to learn to live with this. I thought my life had ended. I became even more angry with God. How could God allow this to happen to me? How could I live this way for the rest of my life?

When I start the day with a low noise level, I try to go about my regular routines. One is to attend church. On a particular Sunday night, I was sitting in the corridor trying to override the chirping in my ears when the pastor sat down by my side. When he asked me why I was in the hallway, I fell apart and explained my situation.

He had no idea but offered to meet for prayer, encouragement, and support. This is one benefit of attending a church regularly and having a pastor who knows who you are and cares. My questions were unanswerable but his concern was what I needed at that time. I eventually had to stop attending all together because any change in noise levels would send my ears blaring and raging.

The tinnitus was another effect of the accident, which resulted in neck surgeries and nerve damage. I was desperate and began trying self-cure. I tried everything advertised that promised to help or even cure. Nothing. I slipped into a state of depression. This is different from discouragement or despair. Depression is a deeper darker place of blue.

I thought no one could possibly understand. My family tried. My friends slipped away because my days were unpredictable and I never knew if I would be able to be with them. They finally quit calling to check on me. I felt alone and rejected. I cried every day.

I began to have suicidal thoughts. That is the darkest blue place to be but I knew I could not go that route. I had to hang on. As a Christian, I knew in my heart that God was listening. I cried out to God to take away the thoughts of suicide and He did. I knew He had a plan for me in spite of all this mess.

Any type of outside noise will set my ears off and make the chirping much worse so I sit at home 99 percent of the time. I cannot pre-plan because I never know what condition my ears will be in when I wake up in the morning. My days continue to revolve around my ears.

This has been a long path. Days have turned into weeks, then months, and now years. I had to find a way to manage my life around the tinnitus.

My pastor, who was so loving and caring, retired in order to care for his wife, who was dying of cancer. One day, I was able to go to their home for a visit. His wife knew about my health situation and commented, "I tried to understand why I had cancer. Then it occurred to me, why not me? I'm no better than anyone else. God gave His Son to die for me, even though I didn't deserve it. He loved me that much." Some months later, she died.

I will never forget our conversation. Her words were uplifting to me and helped me resolve some issues.

My pastor later shared with me the dark-blue place he was in when his wife died. He didn't want to leave the house. He would slip in and out of the church to avoid having to talk to anyone. He said he felt alone.

He then asked me this question, "That describes you, doesn't it?"

I replied, "Your loss is greater because your wife died."

He responded with, "A loss is a loss."

It has now been twenty years since I have walked these dark-blue paths. How did I learn to cope? I start my days by thanking God for His care. I praise Him every day for His grace. He supplies me with all I need.

I stay at home a lot and get lonely sometimes, but I am never alone. There is a difference between being alone or lonely. Being alone is a physical state. Loneliness is an emotional state. God is always present with me.

A verse that has special meaning for me is Deuteronomy 31:8: *"The Lord Himself goes before you and will be with you. He will never leave you nor forsake you. Do not be afraid and do not be discouraged."*

I know God is not finished with me and has a plan still ahead of me. Everything happens for a reason, even when we do not understand. I realize, as I have traveled the dark-blue paths, that I became more aware of the closeness of God. I might not have come to that decision if not for walking these paths. I have learned a lot.

My words of advice to anyone who reads my story would be:

1. Don't just read the Bible. Look deeply into its treasures.
2. Pray every day. Talk to God. He will bring you comfort and peace.
3. Rely on people who commit to pray over you. Prayer is a driving force to moving back from the dark-blue places into the light.

The path of "blue" may change with the episodes of life. The dark-blue path may seem foreboding and loom with darkness. There may be times that become overwhelming and all-consuming. Never fear! God is near! We need not stay on the path of dark blue.

God can lead you off the dark-blue path into the bright blue. Then you can dwell in contented peace, no matter what situation might come along.

Questions for you to consider:

1. An accident changes lives. Are words necessary or is it enough to offer your presence as a means of support? How?

2. What are some ways to encourage anyone who is walking through a life-altering event or who has experienced an unexpected, life-changing situation?

3. Your presence may be all that is necessary. However, your words of advice and counsel may be needed. Do some people mean well but are insensitive to timing? How is timing important?

7

Trusting through Betrayal

n all of our traveling and meeting thousands of people through ministry, Jerry and I have found that some of the most hurting people in a church are the minister and staff families. They are expected to be everything to everyone in the congregation but often their personal needs are neglected. It is difficult to understand betrayal when it occurs in the body of Christ. Betrayal hurts.

> **Psalm 27:5**
> *"In the day of trouble, He will conceal me in His tabernacle. In the secret place of His tent He will hide me. He will lift me up on a rock."*

Trusting through Betrayal—by JO

Have you ever felt betrayed? It is a terrible experience, especially when you are betrayed by people you had known and been friends with for years. The hurt is even deeper when it is aimed at your husband.

My husband had been the pastor of this particular church for twenty-five-plus years and had always been able to work through challenges that often come with ministry. Then we were attacked. As his wife, I could not believe what was being said and the words that were being used about our family.

I received a phone call one afternoon that I certainly was not prepared for. I could tell by my husband's voice that he was troubled. He was at his office at the church and had just had some unexpected visitors. They said they had made a decision that concerned his leadership and did not suggest praying together or trying to work out a solution. No resolution was suggested because these individuals had already decided. They said "they" had made the decision, with no turning back.

As I sat to think over this, I wondered what had happened to some of the people in our church. What about God-honoring solutions to problems? My husband was the only one in the room who was thinking ahead as to how much damage this would bring to the whole church congregation.

We later learned there had been "secret" meetings to talk about how some positions in the church could be rearranged. The person in question needed more money and more power from the church.

It was a "staff" infection that was spreading.

They didn't blatantly call for my husband to resign but he knew he could not stay in a place with this type of toxic atmosphere. There was no expression of love for his feelings or concern for how this would affect our family, even though my husband had invested years into their lives.

In all my years, I had not experienced so much betrayal and lack of love from other "believers." It brought back pain from my childhood. I felt betrayed when my dad left our family and gave us no support or love. These same hurts of betrayal and lack of care came flooding back like huge waves knocking me down.

As my husband had never experienced this type of attack before, he could now understand true betrayal. This was coming from people he had cared for and ministered to. The accusations were unjustified. Obviously, a certain group just wanted control. There were no accusations of immoral or unethical behavior or financial indiscretion, because there were none.

In a church setting, the attack isn't only against the pastor but includes his family as well. Our children were hurt after watching their parents go through this pain. In this situation, it revolved around evil influences that had moved into our congregation with the purpose of destroying the fellowship and taking over the church. It may seem unbelievable to many people but Satan's main goal is to attack the church, destroy the leadership, and stir up problems in the congregation.

Most people in any church fellowship are easily swayed when the voices speaking are authoritative and powerful. It doesn't seem to matter that it often reveals that these people are immature and have a shallow concept of what it truly means to love and serve Jesus Christ. It is usually "their way or the high-way" instead of God's way.

What was my response when I heard what my husband was saying? I said, "Just don't do anything you will regret." I began at that time to pray that God would lead us and that we would respond to His leading. I had invested my life in this church alongside my husband.

I was already beginning to grieve over the loss that I sensed was coming. Each morning I awakened with my pillow wet from my tears. The nights were long with very little sleep, tossing and turning and feeling like it was a horrible nightmare—but it was real. We were being betrayed by people we loved and whom we thought loved us. I read somewhere that the saddest thing about betrayal is it never comes from your enemies; it comes from those you trust.

The next Sunday morning, my husband dressed and, ready for church, said, "Pray that I can preach today." I had never before heard this from him. I was already praying but I needed someone to pray for me that I could get out of bed, get dressed, and walk into the service. I wanted to be with him but I was weak and hurt.

In my desperation, I called a Christian ministry and asked for prayer for my husband and myself. I told them just a little of the situation. The reply was, "You and your husband are in the middle of spiritual warfare." She prayed for strength through this battle and her last words were, "I pray for this wife to not only put on her skirt this morning but also her combat boots." Wow! God used her to help me have strength and I was empowered and ready to be alongside my husband throughout all that was to come.

Spiritual battles may look like flesh and blood but, in reality, the real war is against the powers and rulers of darkness (Ephesians 6:12). But over it all, God showed His power that morning as my husband preached.

My husband knew that God was leading him to resign and we both had peace over the decision. The pain still runs deep and I still grieve. It has been eight plus years and it still hurts.

What are some lessons I have learned? I learned there are people who will be used to destroy and do not care about the fallout. I learned that God is stronger and is made perfect when we are at our weakest.

I learned that forgiveness is a necessity to healing from betrayal. Forgiveness doesn't necessarily have to be reciprocated. It is part of recovery and restoration.

I also learned that God's grace will carry you when you are breaking. It will take you from the dark-blue place of despair and pain back to a brighter place of healing. It was God's grace that helped me to truly trust God, even through betrayal.

I learned that one of the loneliest positions in ministry can be as the pastor's wife and kids. People often forget that we are not perfect. We are humans with feelings.

I hurt for the kids of ministers. Some people wonder why many of them walk away from church when they are older. It may be due to their not being able to get past the agony and hurt. My prayer is for those kids to find a place where they can worship in a loving church. Church is still an important place to find support and encouragement.

My final lesson is that no matter what comes my way, I need to conform to the image of Jesus. He was betrayed at the highest level of anyone who ever lived. To be made more like Jesus isn't always going to be a pleasant experience. The trials of life are a test. They will make you better or bitter. I would never want to hurt another person, but I am human.

A verse that helps when I feel the old hurt coming on is Luke 6:27–28: *"Jesus said, 'Love your enemies, do good to those who hate you, bless those who curse you and pray for those who mistreat you.'"* When I read this verse, God uses it in my life to convict me of what I must do. My prayer is, "Lord Jesus, You were wounded and hurt. You know my pain. Please help me not to hurt others even when they hurt me. Thank You, Jesus, for being willing to be despised and shamed. In doing that, You have shown every person the meaning of true forgiveness. Help me to always offer forgiveness as Your servant. Give me tough skin and a tender heart, and help me to love other people as You love me."

Psalm 56:11
"In God I trust. I will not be afraid. What can man do to me?"

Questions for you to consider:

1. Have you ever felt betrayed? Can you share your experience?
2. Did you come to a place of acceptance and how did that happen?
3. Betrayal comes in many forms. How would you encourage the person who feels they have been betrayed?
4. Can you recall from the Bible the different ways Jesus was betrayed?
5. Jesus was the perfect example of what betrayal looks like and the way to move through the hurt and pain. How?

8

The Blue of Pain and Hurt

People can be deceptive in the way they present themselves to others. What is observed on the outside may not be what is boiling in the inner person. Every choice has a consequence. The consequences of poor choices have a ripple effect like a stone thrown into a pool of water. It begins with a small plop in the water but the circle widens in the aftermath.

> **James 1:14**
> *"Each person is tempted when he is carried away and enticed by his own lust. Then when lust has conceived, it gives birth to sin and when sin is accomplished it brings forth death."*

The Blue of Pain and Hurt—by C

The pain and hurt were so deep I thought my heart would explode. Despair gripped my heart as my precious son buried his head in my chest and wept. "I'm sorry, Mommy. I didn't know Daddy had secrets and that he is gay." I held him tightly and let him sob endlessly. I had kept the total truth from my boys until I had to tell them.

Just one year earlier, I knew my marriage would disintegrate. Pornography is a gateway into an evil, dark-blue world. My husband became addicted to internet pornography. He neglected me and the boys and every day after work he would go directly to his computer. It took me a while to realize what was happening. I thought he might just need some "down" time and had no idea that he was getting more deeply involved in the perverse side of porn.

When I finally confronted him, he denied that he needed help so I had to take action. I had no idea how to raise our boys but knew it was now up to me. First, I had to protect their young hearts from the truth about their Dad's porn addiction.

I carried this burden with limited family help except for my Mom. She did what she could while dealing with personal health issues and cancer treatment. I sank further into despair and depression. As a nurse, I could barely provide for our needs so took weekend work, as it provided better pay.

As I told the boys the truth about their dad being involved in internet pornography, I cried from the deep, dark-blue place in my heart. I held my oldest son, who is more expressive, and listened to him rage. He could not understand how this had happened. Then I watched as my youngest son, still sweet and innocent regarding the harshness and cruelty of the world, tried to process what he had just learned. It was hard for all of us to believe this about their daddy. My youngest son is quiet and reflective but I could tell that both my boys were trying to make sense of all this. We were entering a time of dark blue. As I went to bed that night, I knew we were all numb and in pain and agony.

I have to admit I became confused and angry with God. I was desperate and I thought I had come to the end of my rope. My questions were, "How, God, could You allow this to happen? Why has my marriage not only ended, but in such a tragic way?" I had prayed for thirty-eight years that the Lord would send me a godly man, a spiritual leader, a lasting marriage and a God-filled home.

The home my brother and I grew up in was torn apart by divorce, too. Divorce not only tears apart the family, it leaves scars on every heart. I did not know this was just the tip of the iceberg for the three of us.

One year later, I was struggling to live paycheck to paycheck and trying to hold together what was left of our family. The boys were seeing their father every other weekend. Just when I thought things couldn't get worse, they did.

I learned that my ex-husband and his boyfriend had moved in together. I found out from my boys that the boyfriend was verbally abusive to my sons. Back to court we went to be certain that my boys did not have to endure any more hurt. This resulted in their father pulling away from them. I'm glad in the divorce settlement he was required to give some financial support. Other than what the court mandated, he stopped additional financial help.

During the chaos of those six years, I continued to date periodically. As I began to think about any future relationships, I set standards and boundaries on which I would not compromise. I wanted to find a man who would become a godly mentor for my boys. They needed a stable, caring man who would be an example of what a husband and father should be.

Every man I dated just didn't meet my nonnegotiable list of what I wanted in a lasting relationship. Even men that some of my friends recommended as "a catch" just didn't meet the standard. I decided that never again would I settle for less than what God wanted for me. (An interesting fact is my ex-husband and I had dated through high school and college. He was highly thought of and no one would have ever suspected that he had underlying secrets that would eventually come to light.)

The blue of life was dark and was consuming me, but I clung to God's Word, even though I was still angry. I relied on older, wiser women who prayed for me and my boys. These became my strongholds.

We also found a Christian counselor who was able to help me keep what little sanity I had left and helped me and my boys work through so many areas of hurt and pain. Oh, yes, and anger.

One area of regret is that, due to the financial needs requiring me to work on Sundays, I could not attend church. I missed that. There is something fulfilling about the worship experience, support, and encouragement you can only find in a church setting. The inability of being able to attend church left me drained spiritually. I just resorted to pleading with the Lord to let me sense His working and to restore us to a brighter-blue place from this darkness. I spent countless hours in tears, begging God to remove the thorn of loneliness and spiritual dryness I was feeling.

Then, in 2021 I had a breakthrough. I surrendered all my hurt and pain to the Lord. I opened my heart and laid my personal will and dreams over on the shoulders of my heavenly Father. I knew He loved me and cared but I had not trusted Him enough to release all this to Him. I changed my prayers to "Lord, Your will, not mine!"

In April 2022, a friend suggested I check out a Christian dating site. I was reluctant and literally had no desire. I decided to take the advice basically out of curiosity.

I posted. Two weeks later, I received a sweet message from a man who actually lived close by. He went to church regularly and played the drums in his church praise team.

I ran this by my sons and our counselor and found that my counselor knew him. They approved of my meeting him. With some hesitation, I accepted a lunch invitation. As we shared, I learned that he, too had been hurt in his former marriage.

We began dating and as we prayed together, I listened to him open his heart not to me, but in prayer to God. He was transparent and respectful. He honored the boundaries I had set and allowed me time to get to know him better. We both didn't need to rush into a new relationship.

We needed time to get acquainted.

Due to my past childhood experience with the trauma of divorce, he offered to go with me to counseling and pay for it, too. We are still in counseling together. This allowed us to draw closer. When we became engaged, I knew that God was honoring all my prayers and pleading. God brought this man straight to me and I knew it, though I was still gripped with fear from what both of us had experienced in our previous relationships.

Once I faced my fears, I agreed to marry him. He is truly the man I prayed for from childhood. He is the spiritual leader of our home and gives love unconditionally. I had almost come to the conclusion I would never find this man this side of Heaven.

Wow! God gave me the man I prayed for and a new job, too. We all attend church together: him, me, my boys, and his two little girls. We watch him in the praise team. Little did I ever expect that, along with my two boys, I would be given the blessing of being the "other mother" to two girls. There are new challenges when you blend families, but with the overseeing guidance of God and a godly man who is attentive to God's leading, it can be done.

There were times when I didn't have any words to pray. I cried out from my place of personal hurt and pain. A scripture that is dear to me is found in Romans 8:26–28:

> "The Spirit of God helps us in our weakness. We do not know for what we ought to pray but the Spirit Himself intercedes for us with groaning and words that we cannot express. He who searches our hearts knows the mind of the Spirit because the Spirit intercedes in accordance with God's will. We know that in ALL things God works for the good of those who love Him who have been called to His purpose."

We all have dark-blue valleys we must face before we can move into a brighter-blue place. When I couldn't sense God's presence, I still knew in my heart He was working. The dark blue has lifted and we are now returning to a much brighter place for our entire family.

> **Romans 12:2**
> *"Do not conform any longer to the pattern of this world, but be transformed by the renewing of your mind."*

Questions for you to consider:

1. Do you know of any person who is dealing with homosexuality? How does this affect the people and relationships around them?
2. Do you think that homosexuality is a choice? What would the Bible say about this issue?
3. Are there degrees of sin? Explain your answer.
4. Is there any recourse for a person who is living a homosexual life style or for a child who has changed their gender?
5. What would you say to the person who is attempting to work through the reality of what lies ahead when this is exposed?

9

Behind the Scenes

Every family has a history. In small communities, people usually know most everything that is going on. It's interesting that, although there is a family history for a Christian, the family history is not nearly as important as the realization that our family history can be part of History!

God has a plan that sometimes leads families down interesting paths, some with beauty all around. Other parts of the path may reveal the unexpected scene that lies ahead.

> **Luke 1:1**
> *"A record of the genealogy of Jesus Christ the son of David, the son of Abraham."*

Behind the Scenes—by R

When I started thinking about how I would begin my story, I was reminded of a quote that has stayed with me for many years: "Our life is an open book. We write in it daily."

When we attend a play, we see only the curtain—until it is opened. Then we can see the scenes behind the curtain. Our lives are like that. Future experiences are hidden behind the curtain until they are made clear. People see what is on the outside, but there are scenes lying below the surface. My story is an open book and as I reveal what lies behind the curtain of my life, I pray it will be a source of encouragement to you when you face a dark-blue place in your life.

Life is filled with storms. These episodes sometimes take the breath out of life. It is very important to learn how to return from a dark-blue stormy place in our lives to a lighter, brighter place.

I was raised on country sunshine—a farm girl and proud of it. My sisters and I worked on the farm. Lots of memories.

I attended a small school where I met a young boy. He worked on his family farm so we had a lot in common. We were school friends, then it blossomed into love and marriage.

We believed marriage to be for life and committed this to each other. We expanded our family by two daughters and a son. We decided early in our marriage that family and church would be our priorities.

The first storm came when our son was diagnosed with Hodgkin's Lymphoma. After twelve chemo and thirty radiation treatments, we entered a dark-blue time. Afterward our son, P, developed complications. We worked through this but there were many dark-blue days.

With every storm of life there come moments and sometimes days of questioning. The blue days can become dark and overwhelming, especially when it involves your children.

After moving through P's health crisis, we all resumed daily life. Then another storm hit. P was in a car accident that resulted in a broken neck. We heard the doctor say that this type of neck injury usually ends in paralysis or even death. We prayed and, after six months our son began to recover.

H and I struggled with so many questions. "How can we go through much more, Lord?" Then the answer came. We began to sense a surrounding of God's presence. We decided to find areas for which to be grateful. This moved us "through" and back into a brighter-blue place.

We found that as we turned to God with a thankful heart, He gave us joy, which overrides any adversity. As joy returned, so did God's peace: *"When troubles of any kind come your way, consider it an opportunity for great joy"* (James 1:2–3).

Our son began to volunteer at the sheriff's office, and then was hired. The sheriff didn't think he could pass the physical tests but he did. He worked in law enforcement for ten years and became Assistant Police Chief.

Then another storm came. One morning P didn't show up for work. The Chief went to check on him and found him lying face down, unresponsive. Results indicated a brain bleed with the probability of no recovery. Our hearts were again heavy and in a dark-blue place. Miraculously, P lived through surgery and had no speech problems, but his short term memory was affected. He could no longer work. Going from extremely active to inactive creates a whole new paradigm.

In spite of all the crises he went through, P lived to see his two daughters grow up, marry, and give him grandchildren. This made us great grands.

H and I lost our only son in 2017. Mothers aren't supposed to outlive their children We were learning as a family that in the good days or bad days, God is in all days. God uses heartache for His good. Our faith grew stronger even through our grief.

After his death, we learned more about how P was able to move through the dark days he experienced. He relied on Scripture. His favorite Bible passage was 1 Corinthians 13. He wrote in his Bible, "This is so true to live a more peaceful and perfected life. This kind of love will carry you through anything."

Another storm was coming. Our youngest daughter was diagnosed with breast cancer. I thought my heart would explode. Again I asked, "How much more can we take?"

H said, "God will see us through." And He did.

Even though I was stuck in hurt, and as tears flowed, my heart continued to be renewed through Scripture and music. The song, "God on the Mountain," reminded me that the God of the good times is still God in the bad times.

After months of treatment and now ten years later, our daughter is cancer free. She said, "As long as God leaves me here on this earth, I feel He wants me to spread His Word to others." She does this as a school nurse.

How many dark-blue storms can any family go through? Another storm was looming just ahead.

I was given a blessing when I married my husband, H. He was the love of my life for sixty-two years. We walked hand in hand. We told each other, "I love you" morning and night. He was a great man of God, husband, and father.

He awoke one morning in severe pain. The diagnosis revealed an esophageal tear that caused fluid to build up in his whole body. Emergency surgery was performed with little hope of recovery. I felt like my heart had left my body.

I was existing with a broken-down, hurting heart. I couldn't sleep and couldn't see any way out. One sleepless night, I looked across the hospital room and saw our two beautiful daughters. I thanked God for this blessing.

It may sound trite, but again I was reminded that when we can find a way to be thankful, God will restore a sense of His peace. Even when the days are the darkest blue, God has a brighter-blue place waiting.

The Scriptures that constantly remind me of His promises are found in James 4:8 and Psalm 9:9–10:

"Come near to God and He will come near to you"

"The Lord is a refuge for the oppressed. A stronghold in times of trouble. Those who know your name trust in you, for you Lord, have never forsaken those who seek you."

H never fully recovered and passed away in 2019. I had lost our only son and now H was gone, too. Family and friends were a source of support. A friend brought a plaque that still hangs on my wall: *Be still and know that I am God* (Psalm 46:10).

As I watched the love of my life slip away, I grieved. I prayed hard for God to help me. With God's help, I have survived through the darkest of blue. Everywhere I turned there was a saying or scripture that strengthened me. My girls, the grandchildren, friends, and even strangers offered just the right words when I was having a dark-blue moment and thought I couldn't possibly go on.

The question remains, "How can anyone return to a brighter-blue place in life after such experiences?" You may not believe in God, but I have found the only permanent place to dwell is under the shelter of God's loving arms.

At the beginning of my story I asked the question, "Why Lord?" I still ask sometimes. It is comforting to know that God always hears and listens. He whispers into my heart the word "through."

As He has led me, he can also lead you "through" the dark-blue places back into the brighter-blue place just as He did me.

The key to God leading us "through" comes as we rely on Him by faith day in and day out. Not just grasping onto Him when the darkest blues come along. A foundation of faith is imperative.

A verse I cling to is Isaiah 43:2: *"When you pass through the waters, I will be with you and through the rivers they will not overflow you. When you walk "through" the fire you will not be burned."* When faith is in place God will carry you back from the darkest blue places into the brighter blue.

> ### Isaiah 55:12
> *"You will go out in joy and be led forth in peace."*

Questions for you to consider:

1. Have you ever felt overwhelmed by life? How would you suggest for a person who is currently overwhelmed to maintain a positive attitude?
2. How might your personal struggle to cope with a crisis in your life impact other members of your family?
3. How important to you is having a circle of caring friends who pray for you and with you?
4. Have you ever shared a time in your life when you just could not make sense of the situation?

10

The Blue of Broken Pieces

God set a plan for the union of man and woman from the beginning of His creation. He planned for this union called marriage to be for a lifetime. It required a determined commitment from both man and woman.

According to statistics, one half of all marriages will end in divorce. This rate is higher with second marriages. The reasons for divorce are varied with the most common reason being lack of commitment, followed by infidelity.

Divorce does not only have an effect on the marriage but alters the dynamics of the entire family.

> ### Matthew 19:8
> "Jesus replied, 'Moses permitted divorce because of the hardness of man's heart. But it was not this way from the beginning.'"

The Blue of Broken Pieces—by MM

Although the pandemic had taken its toll on so many American families, I was trying to make the best of the situation. I had bought a business, releasing me from my nine-to-five job. It was the opportunity of a life time but then the hammer fell. It became the hardest year I'd faced since entering the work force in 2004.

I'll never forget the comment of my then-five-year-old daughter, "Maybe Mommy will love you now" she said. I had brought a gift to her on a random occasion. Not only my business but my family was taking the impact of the pandemic. I was struggling to make it all work.

Communication with my wife became sparse. Any attempt was ignored or brushed aside. I came home from a hard day at work to have her say to me, "We need to talk." She said she had decided we needed to divorce because she had thought everything out and knew we were done. She said, "Nothing will help." I was blindsided. I knew things weren't perfect but I was stunned by "her" decision. She wanted no input from me. No discussion.

Perhaps I had always made the decisions for our family and maybe she thought this was one she could make on her own—and she did. I was frozen in place. I thought about our five- and two-year-old daughters, and how all that we had been building since our marriage in 2007 was coming to an end. Just like that and I had no say.

We went for counseling. In the first two sessions, my wife pointed out all the things I didn't do. After two sessions, she said she was done; her mind was made up and she was sticking to it. I continued to go to counseling for support and to seek guidance on how to navigate this disaster. I wanted to hold on to my family that we had made over 13 years of marriage.

Over the next few months, I did note a drastic change in her. She would seem to reach out with statements like, "If you would only do this," or, "I tried to tell you, but you just didn't listen."

The next five to six months were the most painful of my life. I just knew that things weren't right. I slept on the couch as she locked our bedroom door. I thought I was giving her some space and this would help. Things continued to be more tense. I even tried the "love/dare" approach. I tried every means possible as I tried to build a bridge back. Even though I tried, every bridge was knocked down.

I began to see many things that were out of place. She was secretive and hid things.

She would go to "visit" her family or "sister" more than usual. When I had to work long hours to keep the business going, she would take the kids to her parents so she could "figure things out." Her work schedule and time off didn't match. I smelled smoke on her clothes even though no one in our circle of family smoked. I sensed she was talking to someone at work. It was true. I overheard her say, "He says he loves me but…." Cameras in our home did confirm her frequent phone calls.

My counselors gave me strength to set boundaries and be firm as a leader in our home. I think I had lost my role as the leader of our home and my attempts at that point were failing. Confrontation turned defensive. She refused to show me her phone or to answer questions. I kept watching and asking questions.

I was trying to find ways to deal with all the stuff. I kept a "war room" like in the movie by that name. I wrote prayers and verses on the wall. I listed things for which I needed to ask for her forgiveness. I prayed on my knees daily. I asked God to restore my marriage. I just wanted my family back. Even after finding out about her affair, I continued to pray because I knew God could do anything. I knew it was His will for us to have an intact family.

Our pastor talked us into going to a marriage retreat. He noted to my wife that, no matter what happened, she would always have a relationship with me and our children and future grandchildren. She agreed to go.

Before the retreat, she planned a birthday party for me. It was a get together but seemed really off. On the way home from the party, she looked down at her phone and then quickly moved it. I glanced and saw flirty emoji texts. I didn't say anything as I knew we still had the retreat coming.

On the morning we were to leave for the retreat, she had supposedly worked the night before and was sleeping in. I went to get her up and was yelled at, cussed, and screamed at for waking her up. I called a Marriage Helper who tried to coach me as to what to do. I reluctantly packed our car for the trip to the retreat. As we drove, she just looked out the window as if she were about to break down in tears.

On the second day of the conference, I received confirmation that my wife had been having an affair with someone from work. She broke down and told me that she had gone to see him the night before and found him dead. She was supposed to be working.

After the conference, there seemed to be some remorse and sorrow. It may have been due to his abrupt death or the conference. Either way, it seemed to be getting better. She was being more open.

About a month later, I received a text message asking me if I liked the fact that my wife was seeing other men. I confronted her and learned that she was now seeing the cousin of the man that died. At this point, I told her to leave. Our family could not and would not stand for this.

We had a couple we'd been friends with for several years. She told them everything and it seemed she wanted to make things right and for our marriage to recover. But, sadly, sometimes you can't trust even friends you have known for years. The couple we had been friends with deceived me and took advantage financially and personally. They tried to make it up but it destroyed our long-time friendship.

I was drained. I decided to finally give in to her demands for a divorce. I settled with her in order to keep things from dragging through court.

Because I thought I was doing what God wanted, I gave her a fair share of our possessions, the home equity, and money we had invested in the business. I even agreed to equal time with the children again to avoid having to involve the court system.

I continued to pray trusting that God had a plan. What? Would my family be put back together and my wandering wife come home? I didn't know.

I had tried to hold on to any last straw. I had moved into a dark place and yet I tried to hang on to what wasn't meant to be.

After the dust settled, I reconnected with some of my childhood friends. I continued to pray and trust in God's plan for me. My friends suggested I begin to date. I gave it a try but learned that "if it ain't what God really wants for you, don't go looking for it." I spent lots of wasted time looking in all the wrong places.

Since I decided this wasn't the route for me, I deleted all the apps on dating from my phone. I knew God had the right person meant for me to meet. I knew God never disappoints on His promises and He wants to bless a home; I just didn't know what that would look like.

As I was deleting the apps, I received a notification from a Christian dating site. It said, "One new match for you." I showed my friend my phone and said, "Should I?"

He replied, "What can it hurt?"

God is a mysterious God, a loving God, a good God! I now truly under-stand what He means by His ways, not ours.

All the times I had prayed for a family, I just thought the one I already had was "the one." I was trying to hang on but God's plan was already working ahead of me.

Sometimes in marriage, someone steps out of God's will. At that point, God is still working His mysterious plan. More often than not, we don't understand at that time.

I met a lady with a similar story to mine. She had been married for thir-teen years, a marriage that ended with her spouse cheating. Her attempts to keep her marriage together failed, just like mine. We had both been willing to do whatever was necessary to keep our marriages together, but neither of us were successful.

We began dating and she and I both kept going for individual counseling, which eventually led to us going together. There are always areas which need an objective viewpoint. Our counselor helped us address personal issues which needed our attention in order for us to have a healthy relationship.

God is a master storyteller. For both our stories, God brought our broken pieces together. Since He has put us together, it is better now than ever before.

Only God can put broken pieces together to create a family that has His blessing.

My word of encouragement is keep trusting. Never give up on God's ultimate plan. A verse that is special to me is Psalm 147:3: *"He heals the brokenhearted and binds up their wounds."*

> ### Psalm 54:4
> *"Surely God is my help the Lord is the one who sustains me."*

Questions for you to consider:

1. What might be some emotions that are experienced when divorce is inevitable?
2. Since God created marriage to be for a lifetime, how do we explain the current trends in the dissolution of marriages?
3. How do you console children when divorce becomes a reality?
4. In your opinion, how should the Church address the area of divorce?

11

The Dark Blue of the Wilderness

S udden assaults are on the increase. Fear grips our nation. Women especially sense unrest when they go out of their homes even to go buy groceries or shop.

The fear of being assaulted is real. The attack leaves deep scars and remaining feelings of unrest that are often carried through life.

> **Psalm 97:10**
> *"Let those who love the Lord hate evil for He guards the lives of His faithful ones."*

The Dark Blue of the Wilderness—by BW

There was a desperate cry emanating from a terrible wilderness. It was the deep, agonizing cry of a broken heart surrounded by foreboding, dark-blue clouds that never allowed tears relief to rain down. That cry was from a place deep in my soul.

When I was seven years old, Jesus became my very best friend. I knew He was always with me. He knew my secrets. We walked hand in hand every day. He was an ever-present peace in my life. I rested in my sleep—secure, safe, and content in His care.

One day, as a young adult, I was out strolling—enjoying my relationship with Jesus, looking at the trees, and listening to the birds singing. I walked until almost dusk.

The next morning, I awakened in alarm and despair. I felt surrounded by a dark-blue cloud of impending doom. This eerie experience left me feeling that Jesus was gone.

As I asked, "What is this place?" I prayed and it seemed as though my prayers were bouncing back unanswered "Where are you, Jesus?" I only felt grief, confusion, fear, depression, and a sense of loss.

That year was a time of searching, crying out, and occasional feelings of despair. I felt a spiritual dryness. The bright blue of life had become dull, lifeless, and dark.

I remember saying, "Well, if Jesus is gone, I might just live it up on Earth." Then, just as quickly, my heart said, "I don't want to do this, Lord. I want to live for You." So that's what I did, but I was just going through the motions. I read my Bible, but with no feelings. My prayers fell back in my face. I went to church but my worship felt empty.

Then God showed me Exodus 13:17–18: *"When Pharaoh let the people go, God did not lead them on the road through the Philistine country though that was shorter. God led them through the desert road toward the Red Sea."*

This scripture made me realize that God might lead us on a longer path so we can learn that we can trust Him and never give up. I knew then that God had not left me but that He would give me strength to keep going on.

There were still months of His silence but I was trusting Him and learning from His words in the Bible. My relationship with God changed from being experiential—"feelings based"—to a faith-based daily walk. I was learning not to be led by my emotions but to exercise my faith.

Years later, I again was crying out to God. He led me again to His word. Isaiah 49:15–16,

> "Can a mother forget the baby at her breast and have no compassion on the child she has borne? Though she may forget, I will not forget you! See I have engraved you on the palm of my hands. You are ever before me."

The next day, as a friend opened her wallet, a card fell out. On it was a picture of a child laying on a huge hand. The card said, "See I have engraved you on My hands."

Throughout the years, I periodically asked God, "What happened that morning?" I again heard no answer. I met my husband, married, and had kids. We bought a house. Life went on.

Finally one year I said in desperation, "God! When I journal my struggles in life, it points me back to that eerie morning. Will you tell me what happened?"

Slowly and gently a memory fell into place. It took me a week to come to the understanding that the memory was a real event. I saw the rape as a violent, physical attack that resulted in trauma that interrupted that beautiful walk with Jesus all those years in the past. As I didn't know what to do with that experience, I went to bed and again buried the memory. I put that trauma to sleep in my mind for thirty-three years.

Since then, my return to a brighter-blue place has been gradual. Bible studies, counseling, and prayer over me have built, brick by brick, a wall of healing. Now that I can look back, I see that God was building, changing, and teaching me. I learned three things:

1. There is a very real spiritual wilderness. People enter it through a variety of circumstances. But God, as our loving Father, allows these experiences as times of testing to make us stronger and more mature.
2. It is very important to continue to trust and obey God's Word even when it seems like a dry place. Keep seeking reading, praying, serving, and being in fellowship with other Christians.
3. A life led simply by feelings is unstable. Faith is a strong leader that endures and always leads with Truth.

The recent thing I have learned is that God is my Rock. Solid and Faithful. His loving kindness will carry me through any hard or traumatic circumstances or hardships. God wants every person to believe His Truth and to know His attributes.

God by His grace and love is the only Hope that will result in returning to a brighter-blue life from any dark-blue place. He will overflow you with His joy and peace and with Hope by His Spirit as you believe in Him.

Psalm 97:11

"Light is shed upon the righteous and joy on the upright in heart. Rejoice in the Lord you who are righteous and praise His Holy Name."

Questions for you to consider:

1. You may not know anyone who has been raped but the probability of knowing someone who has or is experiencing abuse is likely. What words of encouragement might you be able to express?
2. Does a trauma such as this leave permanent scars? How can these scars be minimized?
3. What resources are available in your community to aide women who have been raped or abused?
4. Does your church have an area of support available to help in these situations?

12

Prayer through the Dark Blue

M oving to a new country is daunting. Learning a new language, customs, and traditions are challenging. Finding friends and building relationships are often the first priority when relocating.

Then there is the challenge of where to turn when an unexpected health issue arises.

Being far away from family and friends makes it imperative to find a support system to help and to be encouraging. God is a refuge, strength and guide no matter who you are, where you are from, or whatever you may experience.

Psalm 118:5

"From my distress I called upon the Lord. The Lord answered me and set me in a large place."

Prayer through the Dark Blue — by CI

I am originally from Imo State in Nigeria. My brother and I moved to the US in November 2012 and lived in Maryland for eight years before moving to Missouri. My mum still lives in Nigeria and my sister in Japan.

These past ten years have been a big time of adjustment for me. I have had to learn to navigate life in America with different systems and new experiences. I had hoped these would work for me.

Beginning in 2018, I started to have intense pain with bleeding that lasted for incredibly long periods—sometimes as long as three months with a one-week break between episodes.

The pain was so intense I had to lie in one position for relief. Multiple times I had to have blood transfusions. The diagnosis was always the same. The doctors could not figure out why I was bleeding so much. In 2020, I was back in the hospital.

During this time, I was in an emotionally and verbally abusive marriage. It was exhausting. I finally decided to leave the relationship and put as much distance as I could between myself and my husband. I also quit my nine-to-five job in order to go to nursing school.

The physical and emotional challenges began to weigh on me. I became depressed. I had moved into a dark-blue place in my life that I had not been in before.

The blood transfusions I received helped and, over the next two years, I felt some relief. I thought God had finally come through and my story was only going to get better. I was not prepared for what was coming.

After two more ER visits, a hospital stay, doctor visits, and multiple appointments with gynecologists, on August 11, 2022, I was told I possibly had endometriosis and surgery would be needed to confirm and remove any affected tissue. I imagined the worst-possible scenarios.

I had surgery on August 18. This confirmed the endometriosis, which had spread into the fallopian tubes. These, along with fibroid tumors, were removed during the surgery.

Just before my post-op follow-up appointment, I had my thirtieth birthday. I was feeling really good for the first time in a long time. Then came another shock.

At the post-surgery visit, my doctor told me that they had done tests on the removed tissue and the tests came back positive for cancer cells.

I don't think I heard anything after she said the word "cancer." She referred me for a consultation with a gynecology oncologist who could better diagnose me and give me more guidance. I made it to the parking lot before bursting into uncontrollable tears. I sat in my car for the next hour, crying. A dark-blue cloud was overwhelming me.

I was asked to bring someone with me to the next appointment. There was no one I could ask since I had yet to make friends after my recent move to Missouri. My brother lived a thousand miles away and we weren't very close anyway. I finally asked a cousin, who went with me. At the appointment, I was told how far the cancer had already spread and that it had invaded my ovaries. It was spreading across my liver and abdominal organs.

The doctor talked about treatment options and how aggressive we would need to be. They needed to start immediately. All I could think about was "I'm going to die." I was confronted with so much information. I had so many questions yet didn't have time to think through everything, so I simply said yes to what the doctor suggested.

In discussing some options, I was told that saving my eggs for later pregnancy was not an option. I wanted to have children but that wasn't going to be in my future. This cancer was estrogen dependent and fertility treatments would worsen the condition.

I channeled my feelings of grief, anxiety, and stress into prayer. I cried as I prayed and yelled to God because, in those first four to six weeks, all I could think of was the worst possible outcome to this situation. I told God that if He would let me survive, He would have to stop the cancer from spreading.

I told my mum a month after the diagnosis. I told her she need not worry for me. Her reaction gave me much-needed strength and motivation. Her response was calm as she told me God was going to take care of me and that I would become a testimony of His grace. My mother's words were exactly what I needed.

Three weeks after my diagnosis and two weeks before my first chemo session was to begin, I had a CT scan. The mass on my liver which seemed to be spreading aggressively was gone. This certainly encouraged me to keep on going. The clear scan was my beacon of hope. I hung on to my God for dear life and He did not disappoint.

I stayed in school, which motivated me and helped me mentally to be positive. I needed something to look forward to besides doctor appointments and healthcare calls. My doctors even tried to get my mum a visa so she could come and be with me, but the embassy kept refusing to grant it. I would face this primarily alone.

I was worried about so many things but God was going before me in advance. Sometimes He intervened just in time, at the moment I needed Him. In fact, I was not alone.

I joined a cancer support group (via text) and in reading everyone's stories, I discovered a group of supportive women. I could share my thoughts and feelings with them and this made my life just a little bit easier.

I know I have prayed more in these past thirteen months than I have ever prayed before. Prayer is a way to express the deepest needs of the heart. I found prayer lifted my spirits and increased my faith to trust God even more.

This path on my life journey has helped build my faith, repair my relationship with God, learn what I need to know, and given me boldness to speak up for myself. Even though I have had to walk this path alone physically, God has blessed me with people I now consider my family here in the US. They walk along beside me as my path continues.

The once dark-blue cloud has lifted, due to their love, encouragement, and support.

It has been one year and I have had countless chemotherapy and radiation treatments. I have been poked and had surgery. This has been the hardest season in my life as I have gone through physical, emotional, and financial stress. The path has been rough but I am now in remission. My prayer is to have a very long life to give me time as I continue to sort through my feelings about this entire experience.

Hope, endurance, faith, and trust in God are the keys to staying positive no matter how deep the path might go or how crooked the path might become.

> **Psalm 4:8**
> "In peace I will both lie down and sleep for Thou alone, O Lord, dost make me to dwell in safety."

Questions for you to consider:

1. Do you wake in the night and fret or worry about what is coming in the morning?
2. If you have moved to a new location, what were some challenges you faced or are still facing?
3. What advice would you give to someone who is considering relocating to a new country?
4. Is it difficult to admit if you have made an error in what you were thinking that God was leading you to do?
5. How do you discern God's direction?

13

Rolling On—I'm Still Here

It seems as though the challenges of life become greater as we age. The person who can endure has to find strength and courage.

If you live long enough, you will get old. The older person can benefit the younger because of the life skills they have and the challenges they have endured.

> **Psalm 118:14**
> *"The Lord is my strength and song, and He has become my salvation."*

Rolling On—I'm Still Here—by BJ

Life ain't all fun and games, but I'm still here. I was raised in a rural farming community. We didn't have electricity until after 1950 and our road was either mud or dust. I was raised in a church-going family where my parents were busy and active. I was involved and a leader in the youth group and in leadership during my school years.

Back then we didn't think much about our family situation. My parents were good, hardworking people. We lived in a small house. We eventually were able to move into a bigger house with a bathroom, where I had my own room. I'm sure we had many times when the days seemed to be a bit dark, but we just kept "rolling on." I learned the importance of this as I got older.

Everyone has certain personality traits and I guess I have natural leadership qualities. I was always put in some position of leadership whether in school, church or work. Being a leader challenges every emotion. You have to have strength to make decisions that are necessary but not always positively received. Then there is the stress of having to address a variety of other issues.

As life "rolled on," I married my high school sweetheart and we began our married life. We faced decisions of where we would live and what we might do for a living. Things got rocky for a bit, but I "rolled on."

We increased our family by two little girls. About six months later after our second was born, my wife was killed in an auto accident, which moved my life into a period of dramatic change. A season of dark blue moved through. She had left me with our seven-year-old and six-month-old girls.

How did I move back into a brighter-blue place? I was able to move forward due to dear friends who were my support and encouragement, along with my church family. I realized I now had sole responsibility for our girls. I felt it best for us to move in with my in-laws; we lived with them for several years. Sometimes I found I had to do things I didn't necessarily agree with. Living with in-laws can be complicated.

As my life rolled on, I remarried and we had a child, another girl. Our marriage was full of turmoil—so many disagreements, which finally led to divorce. This was another shift into a shadowing of blue days. However, I "rolled on."

After the divorce and now two marriages, I was again faced with life's decisions. A few months later, I married a lady I had known and been friends with for many years.

During our now thirty-four years of marriage, there have been many challenging times. Changing jobs, health challenges, and family dynamics all contribute to my ongoing stories. Life is filled with ongoing stories, isn't it? Some pleasant. Some not so pleasant.

One monumental experience that has continued to help me "roll on" is my decision to trust Jesus Christ. I had always been involved in church but church isn't the "fix." Church life sometimes has a way of creating a different type of stress. It can be brutal. Living in a small community, there is very little that isn't known. At church, there were times I felt rejected and pushed aside. Due to my personal hurt, we quit going for a while.

Since church has always been important to me, and I found support there during some of my more blue experiences, I was drawn back to church. My wife and I began to attend a local fellowship where we immediately felt accepted.

Feeling valued is vital to being able to "roll on" through the episodes of life. Church offered us value and acceptance.

As I stated, I have leadership qualities that drive me to be more than a pew sitter. I love music, so I joined the choir and volunteered to teach a Bible study class.

One continuing area of concern for me is the relationship I do not have with my third daughter. For all practical purposes, she has disowned me, saying I am a hard man. Family relationships can be hurtful and painful. Trusting that God knows and cares keeps me "rolling on" when I consider what I may be missing with my grandchildren.

Two things stand out as I recall some of those blue times. One is that Jesus is always there. He has my back. Even in the darkest of days, when the clouds cover the sun, the SON is always shining. Also, I reflect on the importance of good friends whose encouragement is invaluable.

As you read my story, you see that I have been through a lot. The secret for me of how to move back from the dark-blue times has been to continue to push through. It ain't been all fun and games, but here I am, still "rolling on."

Now into my eighties, I offer this word of advice: continue on the path that is before you and make the most of the situation at hand. As dark blue enters life, light blue is still ahead. The shift from light blue to dark blue will pass and the light blue will return.

> ### Colossians 1:10–11
>
> "So you may walk in a manner worthy of the Lord to please Him in all respects bearing fruit in every good work and increasing in the knowledge of God. Strengthened with all power, according to His glorious might for the attaining of all steadfastness and patience."

Questions for you to consider:

1. Do you have an aging parent or friend?
2. Have you learned anything from an older person that has been valuable in your life?
3. Take time to read Romans 5:3–5 in your Bible. After reading this passage, and reading the testimony of BJ above, what are your thoughts about perseverance and hope?
4. How can you support an older person if they seem to be slipping into a state of despondency?
5. What would be some ways that assistance can be given to an older person without diminishing their personal dignity and self-value?

14

Flow with the Go

Many young adults have a life plan. They obtain their education and set goals for their lives. The most productive and fulfilled people are those who follow a plan that they feel God has laid before them. This in itself will bring unexpected challenges.

A life in ministry is one of faith and endurance. The challenges may come from any number of areas not experienced in other vocations. The satisfaction for those in ministry is watching how God works through those who have followed Him in obedience. Blessings are the result of obedience to God.

> **Matthew 4:19**
> *"Follow me and I will make you fishers of men."*

Flow with the Go—The Story of J and M

The dark-blue experiences of life were during my younger days. Since my marriage to M, we have had very few dark-blue times in our lives. How can we say this?

We determined many years ago to follow God's path to life and work. We determined that our life would be an adventure. Due to this decision, God has kept us from the deep-blue places that many people go through. One motto is to "flow with the go." I define this as to keep going as the flow of life comes along. Season to season. Year by year. Just keep going.

Several years ago M and I were introduced to a book by a godly physician, Dr. Paul Tournier. In his book *The Seasons of Life,* he makes the comparison of the changing seasons of the year to the stages of life. We immediately applied this to our personal lives and to our life call, the ministry of evangelism. He writes that the early years represent the summer of growth and blossom. Autumn is the time of harvest and gathering and the winter season represents the coming of the end of life.

Although there have been times of challenge in life and ministry, we have made smooth transitions from one season to the other. We have moved from early immaturity to growing to adulthood, aging gracefully, and now to the reality of making a smooth transition to the conclusion of life as traveling evangelists. We decided to allow every season to have its proper place and to continually let each season unfold.

Dr. Tournier's book provided spiritual guidance that helped us set our goal to honor the Lord and to stay true and faithful to our ministry calling. We determined to always be honest, responsive, and totally sensitive to God's timing.

We have accepted the fact of changing seasons and will go on following God as He opens and closes the doors of life. We continue to follow faithfully the changes and developments that have transpired and will continue to come.

One way we have been able to "flow with the go" and be effective and fulfilled in evangelistic ministry is to periodically do self-evaluation. We check our motives to be sure we are maturing in faith and understanding. No harsh condemnation of self, just simply self-examination. We address another area: are we being pleasing to God? We don't want anything more, and nothing less.

In the Bible, Paul writes, *"…we were ready to share with you not only the gospel but our own selves"* (see Acts 20:20; Colossians 1:28–29, 1 Thessalonians 2:7–12). In order to "flow with the go," we decided our work would not become what we were going to do but the reflection of who we were.

Our most oppressive blue times come because of the stressors of life. We have made some mistakes. We have had personal and intellectual questions that have arisen. As the years have passed and looking back, we might not have humanly survived if not for the counsel of seasoned and experienced teachers in ministry. We learned to "flow with the go," taking into consideration the advice given but always asking God what He wanted us to learn.

A deeply concerning area for us in evangelism is the temptation to push doors open or to make pulpit exaggerations in order to advance God's cause in the world. Dr. A. W. Tozer warns of this danger. Our initial goal was and is to be faithful and responsible to God. We have to be on guard against any unwholesome motives.

In any area of life, it is sometimes difficult to stay on target. Distractions can cause a barrier to God's blessings. We have found that as we say no to distractions, seeking to please God and be obedient to Him, we receive His blessings and can "flow with the go" through every adventure and new avenue into which He might lead.

We know that God does not need our help. As we have stayed true to His direction and have allowed Him to direct our ministry, He has opened the doors to international evangelism in ways we never could have dreamed possible.

Most of God's greatest evangelists' names are not even known. Count Zinzendorf, a Christian mission pioneer, gave a word to evangelists as they went forward to preach. He encouraged the discouraged and said, "Your job is to faithfully preach the gospel, die, and be forgotten." We pray that as the years continue to pass and the final season of life comes for us, that we are resolved to "flow with the go"—faithfully and namelessly preaching the gospel—until the very end.

Let me offer a word of encouragement from the words of Paul in the Bible, in 2 Timothy 4:7: *"I have fought the good fight. I have finished the race. I have kept the faith."* In other words, "Flow with the go."

Matthew 28:19–20

"Go therefore and make disciples baptizing them in the name of the Father, Son and Holy Spirit. Teach them to observe all that I have commanded you and lo I am with you always even to the end of the age."

Questions for you to consider:

1. Do you have family or friends who are in specialized ministries?
2. How do you support and encourage them?
3. Many people think that only those in ministry are responsible for sharing about Jesus. How would you respond to this statement?
4. Have you considered that even though you may not have been called into ministry that you have been mandated by Christ to share His love, mercy, forgiveness, and salvation to other people?

15

Moving from Dark to Light

ow do people cope and navigate the tough terrain of life's path? Some paths are bumpy, mountainous, curvy, and treacherous. Others smooth and easy. Some may be threatening and loom with despair. The new reality and challenge may bring a covering or shadowing leading to a path that ends in a cloud of dark blue.

I think about the thousands of people Jerry and I have met through the years—each with stories of life events. Some were free to share and others more reserved and hesitant to unfold their journeys. One thing is certain. Everybody has questions. Questions often flow like a cascade of water.

Some common questions are, "What will be the result of this? How is this going to impact my family, friends, and job? How will my emotions change and will I become a different person?"

The interviews I conducted for this book were not only enlightening but inspirational. Everybody had various ways in which they coped. All were very transparent as they unveiled their story. Now that you have read the stories for yourself, I'm certain you can relate. You have a story of your own.

What I learned from each story was amazing. I discovered there were common threads woven throughout the interviews that revealed the unique yet common ways each person navigated through his or her personal experience. These threads were pivotal in aiding the swing back from the cloudy or dark place to a brighter or lighter place of blue. Whether it was health, relationships, aging, caring for an aging parent, vocational decisions, or any number of other life events, these common threads were plain to see.

I found the first common thread and the most important factor in returning to a brighter-blue place in life from the darkening blue to be **HOPE**.

Hope is an essential basic need and driving motivation that keeps people moving forward. When hope is gone, the results may be disturbing or dire. The difference in how a person moves through from dark blue back to bright blue is if a person has hope. Hope for a brighter time is imperative and gives strength and courage.

The second running component was **CONNECTION**. Each person indicated they had a desire to connect in a spiritual way to a source outside themselves. Those who were Christians stated they began to rely more strongly on the power that comes from God. In Him they found strength and courage.

A personal challenge has a way of calling a person back to the very basics of life. What and who is important?

People who said they did not have a personal relationship with God said they looked for some other avenue to aid them in their challenge. A few said they sought a deeper experience through meditation or the practice of yoga to find comfort and solace.

Some people said they took medication or changed their lifestyles. Others said they worked with a personal trainer, became more physically active, or even sought out mediums to help them work through their issues. Everyone sought peace and comfort from somewhere or someone other than themselves. However, I have found through not only personal experience but in my dealing with people who have encountered deep challenges in their lives, the only place to find comfort, strength, and the ability to move forward is in a strong connection with God through a personal relationship with Jesus Christ.

The third common thread in the interviews I conducted was the importance of **TAKING ONE DAY AT A TIME.**

When in a state of despair, despondency, or depression, it is vital to stay focused. Restoration to that brighter-blue place is the goal. The old saying, "Take one step at a time," is true.

One of my life sayings is "Plan for tomorrow but live today." Looking too far into the future may become daunting. Take one day at a time. Besides, there will be other challenges ahead anyway.

Another mutual theme was **SUPPORT**. A good support system can come from family, friends, a caring church group, or perhaps professional counseling. Any of these resources can add to the speed of restoration.

These common threads were important as I was struggling with my own dark-blue places. There was one idea that kept haunting me. In each of my personal experiences, I had slipped and forgotten my life goal—that being "to help people find a better place in life." Or, I might say a "brighter-blue place." My thoughts kept cycling back to that idea, and that, in order to fulfill my life goal, I too needed to return to the bright-blue place.

INVESTMENT in the lives of people would be the way for me. I had been asking God all the usual questions with no particular answers except that I knew I needed to move from an inner focus to investing in encouraging others. I had become self-consumed.

When any life event brings a challenge, the danger is to become inner focused. It is vital to consider yourself and to seek help but care must be taken not to move into a totally self-consumed state. That is when no one else or nothing else matters.

Invest in the lives of others. There are multiple places to serve. Churches who are involved in mission outreach or community agencies are always looking for volunteers to serve. Serving others takes the emphasis off of "self."

The keys to returning to a brighter-blue place in life are to reach in (get in tune with what you are feeling), reach out (find a place for support and encouragement), then reach up (God is the greatest place to begin restoration).

Not every event of life will bring on an emotional upset. Most people can maneuver through life by taking each day as it comes and can control emotions by using whatever coping mechanisms they have in place.

People usually cruise through life. But what happens when life is interrupted by some unexpected event? This may alter what started out to be regular blue day and shift this into a darker-blue place filled with negative emotions.

One person stated that even though she was normally a bright, sunny person most of the time, the events of her life had beaten her down into a place of darkness. This lady's answer to her dilemma was to renew the relationship with Christ which had begun very early in her life. Through this review, she came to the conclusion to put new trust in the promises of Jesus in the Bible. He said in John 16:33, *"I have told you these things, so that in me you may have peace. In this world you will have trouble. But take heart! I have overcome the world."*

If you find yourself in a similar situation, it would be advised take a look at your relationship with Christ and reconfirm who He is to you, and what His promises are.

Questions for you to consider:

1. At the opening of this chapter, there were some common questions identified. When you are going through a dark time, ask them of yourself:
   - *What will be the result of this?*
   - *How is this going to impact my family, friends, and job?*
   - *How will my emotions change and will I become a different person?*
2. Can you identify with the five themes mentioned in this chapter: hope, connection, taking one day at a time, support, and investment? Which ones do you sense God leading you to take note of in your personal life situation?
3. How might these have a positive impact on your answers to question number one above?

16

Attitude Is Everything

I n my professional career in family ministry with Jerry and as a social worker, I have learned that people sometimes have a hard time moving back from a dark-blue experience into a brighter-blue place. The blue days of life need not hang around for long periods of time.

There may be no reasonable explanation to what causes despair. For some people, every day is dark blue. For others, the blue days may come from just one experience. Some people can bounce back quickly, while for others their blue day may stretch into weeks, months, or even years.

Attitudes can have an impact on the whole family. The old adage, "If Mama ain't happy, ain't nobody happy" is so true in that, as women, we have the power to control the emotional atmosphere of our relationships, particularly our family relationships.

Most women suffer from "blue days" monthly. Normally, the monthly "blues" are tolerated and chalked up as part of being a woman. This isn't depression.

Another medical issue is post-partum depression, which many women experience after the birth of a child. In most cases, this passes over a period of time. Ask your doctor for help when this occurs.

Stress, pressure, or disappointment can cause emotions to spin out of control. The talons of dark blue may grab hold and hang on. This spiral may lead to depression.

Just "a bit of blue" left to itself has the potential to become a major emotional and physical problem. Note the phrase "left to itself." The question may become, "Is there any solution? What can I do?" The emotional shift may be almost undetectable.

If you are becoming overwhelmed with some issue in your life, do not be too proud, embarrassed, or shy to ask for help. Talk to your spouse, a family member, or a trusted friend. You can also find help through your church, community, or private practice. There are trained, sensitive professionals available to help you.

Do not allow the dark blue to overwhelm you. Stay vigilant until you have a resolution and can return to a brighter place of blue.

Psalm 116:1
"I love the Lord for he heard my voice. He heard my cry for mercy. Because He turned His ear to me I will call on Him as long as I live."

Questions for you to consider:

1. Where do you find comfort when you are sad?
2. Can you sense when your emotions are returning to a brighter-blue place and what it took to return you to that spot?

17

The Progression of Blue

Psalm 147:11

"The Lord delights in those who fear Him, who put their hope in His unfailing love."

learned the progression of "blue" from a lady who had reached her limit.

Her hair was immaculate, her outfit chic and trendy and her nails neatly manicured. She was articulate. When she introduced herself, there was darkness in her voice. As I searched her face and looked into her eyes, I noted that she was hesitant to return my focus.

She engaged me in conversation, careful not to reveal to much personal information. She asked without making eye contact, "Do you talk with many women who suffer from depression? I can't seem to be able to get a handle on my emotions. They just run wild and my whole family is beginning to suffer because of my attitude and actions. I always thought I could handle anything but lately I am overwhelmed."

She stopped as though she had said too much and then took a deep sigh, one of those sighs that reaches down into the body. As she began to apologize for taking my time, I touched her right shoulder.

Immediately, a tear formed in the corner of her eye and I asked if she would like to sit and talk for a few minutes. As we sat down, she dropped her head into her hands and began to weep. She said, "I can't sleep, I don't eat right, and I feel like crying most of the time. My husband is becoming withdrawn, because he doesn't know quite what to do with me and our children are confused. They are precious and try really hard to be helpful. I am at my wit's end."

On another occasion, I met a lady who had become so depressed that she had lost all hope. She had spiraled into depression, beginning with a variety of health issues. She had exhausted her resources to find solutions to her health problems, but in learning of her history, I noted that she had a history of depressive episodes beginning in her youth. I learned that her mother suffered from depression.

Sometimes there is a direct link from generations past to present mental or emotional situations. Research has confirmed this. In other cases, depression may be linked to life crises, trauma, or experiences, as is true with PTSD (Post-Traumatic Stress Disorder).

Exploring the history of a person is imperative to the total analysis of emotional illness, asking questions such as, "How long have you experienced depression? Where do you think this may have begun?"

If it is determined that the home environment was unhealthy, or a parent was withdrawn, depressed, or emotionally unstable, then this makes an indelible impression. What a child sees and hears certainly has significant influence on the emotions. The result may be emotional instability as an adult.

A trained capable counselor will be able to determine if depression is serious enough to warrant more in-depth treatment. The dark place of depression is treatable but involves a process.

The Four Ds

Despair, Despondency, Discouragement, Depression. Everyone has blue days, some darker than others. For some people, every day is a dark-blue day. They live in the negative. For others, the blue days may come from just one experience.

Despondency can quickly grow into depression.

If you are sensing a slide into a darker-blue place that is out of the ordinary for you, do not hesitate to seek help. Do not allow the dark blue to overwhelm you. Stay vigilant until you have a resolution and return to a brighter-blue place.

Even if you are not in the darkest-blue place, it is important to stay focused on one day at a time. Dark-blue days do not have to overtake you. Let those who love you help. It will encourage them and help you appreciate the value of family and friends.

If you choose to seek professional help, seek out someone who is not only trained in their field but sensitive spiritually. Many times it takes months to recover, especially from a deep depressive episode.

Professionals may have to prescribe medication to assist as you recover and this may take time and patience to see results. Finding the right mix of meds to match the level of your depression, coupled with your physical and psychological makeup, requires working with professionals who are sensitive to each of these crucial areas.

If residential treatment is suggested, that may be exactly what is needed. The goal is to learn how to manage the emotions. A struggling person must decide what they are willing to do to return to a brighter-blue place rather than allowing the dark blue to rule their life.

Another issue is how to pay for treatment. Available insurance to cover the treatment may put limits on the number of sessions you are allowed. No matter the cost, finding treatment that restores mental, physical and emotional and spiritual health is the goal. There is no price too high for returning to a brighter-blue place in life.

What is the nature of blue? You can go to a local paint store and look at all the different hues of blue. It is amazing. You'll find every shade of blue from the palest to the darkest. Even the sky can have different shades of blue! A bright, sunny day can lift the spirits whereas dark clouds or the dark of night may usher in a change in emotions.

Despair may return simply because of a shift in personal circumstances such as a life crisis, trauma, illness, or death. I like the fact that there is a bright side even to the darkest of blue. Don't you? Sometimes the return to a brighter place seems impossible.

A tendency to live in the dark-blue places may be part of the personality makeup. Have you ever known anyone who always seems to look at life with the attitude of "Oh, woe is me." Can this type of person change?

Sometimes blueness comes in slowly or it can just blind side a person. Sudden tragedy or crisis, or, like me a sudden health diagnosis of cancer, can begin a spin or plunge from bright blue to dark blue.

Every person will experience the dark blue places in life at some point. The issue isn't *if* but *what* do you do *when* you experience them? We need to learn to ask, better sooner than later, *Where did this come from and how do I move away from the dark blue to a brighter-blue place? How do I end this emotional rollercoaster?*

No matter where the dark blue begins, there is victory to be had and a return to bright blue is within reach. It is a process. It may take time. A lot depends on you.

Questions for you to consider:

1. Do you know how much influence your childhood home had on you and how much influence you have on your home now?
2. Try this experiment: Pick a day to purposefully be negative and sad. See the responses and reactions you receive.
3. Where would you turn as your first line of defense when in need of help?
4. Do you know what has contributed to where you are today? Did you have a parent who was often depressed? What was the climate in your home?
5. Who is your confidante?
6. Are you willing to do whatever is necessary to get help?

18

My Personal Story Continues

My spiral began slowly. I had become self-consumed. The shock of cancer sent me into a tailspin. Your spiral may stem from some abuse, neglect, rejection, addictions, or a sudden crisis. No matter what the origin, you and God are still where your healing will begin.

Learning to trust God is a requirement. What then are the steps to coping with and conquering the darkest of blue places? I found a series of steps that, for me, were monumental.

Acceptance

Everyone will experience despair. Some people are just better at dealing with life issues than others.

There are some people who are "Pollyanna" personalities. They tend to see everything as rosy. I'm not judging them. I just think they don't live in the world I live in. Sometimes my world is a carousel. I have a hard time getting off.

On the other hand, some people want to blame God for everything by pointing a finger at Him any time they do not understand what is going on in their lives. I know people (and you do, too) who are constantly making choices that lead to another crisis or drama. They refuse to accept personal responsibility. If they don't blame God, they may look for someone or something else to blame—anyone or anything but themselves.

In our present culture, taking personal responsibility isn't considered as an option. It's easier to put the blame somewhere else; however, there is a ripple effect when blame is shifted. According to the Bible healing begins when personal responsibility is acknowledged.

Health crises have a way of jerking you into reality. I knew I had done nothing wrong to cause my cancer. It just "poof" appeared. But I had questions, like, "Why, God, did You allow this?" I wondered, *Will I allow this cancer to manage me or will I maintain a positive attitude no matter what?"*

Studies have been conducted on the results a positive attitude can have on overall health. Keeping a bright-blue focus is important. It may not be the cure, but it will leave a lasting influence on those you love, your friends, and others.

Accepting that I had been diagnosed with cancer was not easy. My initial response was to be angry and afraid. The more I dwelt on these thoughts, the more I drifted into a darker-blue place. When I finally was able to think a bit more clearly, I found the first step toward my moving away from the dark blue.

That step was to accept and acknowledge where I was and that I was incapable of finding my way out of the dark-blue place alone. I could not conquer and recover by myself. A personal evaluation can be painful but will bring clarity. It takes patience and a desire to seek guidance. I'm not usually a very patient person. I had to address that.

I did not know if I would be healed from cancer, but I did know that I would not allow the physical cancer to become a spiritual cancer. God redirected me and changed my outlook and focus. Did I become more patient? Well, sometimes.

Another question I faced was, "Do I really want to live continually in this dark place?" Some people do. I did not.

There are consequences for the person who chooses to remain continually in the dark-blue place. It will result in other related physical, psychological, emotional, and relational issues.

The dark-blue state will drag not only the person who is in that place down, but will also impact everything and everyone in its path.

People may shy away from the person who is constantly morose. Their circle of friends may grow smaller and they may instead be attracted to others who are in equally dark places. "Birds of a feather flock together." This can be unhealthy.

I did not want to face my situation alone and certainly not from a negative frame of mind, so I had to accept where this might lead and not allow myself to go there. Personal discipline is always hard.

Support groups can be very helpful. The best ones are those where there is leadership that can keep the atmosphere positive and does not allow the participants to leave the group in the same way they arrived. The goal is for encouragement to prevail. The group should be led by experienced, trained, and caring professionals who know how to redirect people away from the dark blue to help them to return to a brighter blue.

There are so many resources available. It may take exploring your area to locate the right place for you to start. I began to look for a support system not only within my family but Also outside of my circle. When you decide to seek help, start by asking God to lead you to the right source and then trust Him to direct you.

I did not want to move further down the path of despair because I knew it would put a division between me and those I love and care about. I wanted desperately for God to use my life and I knew that staying in that dark-blue place would hinder His ability to use me fully.

As I mentioned earlier, when I was diagnosed, the first thing I experienced was anger then fear. These two coupled with the uncertainty of my prognosis moved me back to a former place of dark blue. Despair intercepted a perfectly wonderful relationship with God and my family. But I knew God had not left me, and that my family would surround me.

Returning to the brighter place required me to take a look at my relationship with God and others. I knew what I had gone through before and did not want to return there. I became afraid that this would again drag me down. I also knew, if I became consumed with my fear, how this might affect my healing from cancer.

In His grace and mercy, God offers hope through His Word. He saw me through and will see *you* through, too. He knows our outcome before we ever enter the valley of dark blue. Jerry says, "We are either entering a valley, are in a valley or coming out of a valley. The fact is: a valley is open on both ends." My valley seemed long.

No matter how long the valley seems, I learned that no one has to stay in the valley. We do not have to walk through it alone and there is victory at the other end. I discovered that at the end of the valley is where to find the brighter-blue place. So much I had to accept. Seeking the end of the valley kept me positive.

Confession

Confession is a big Bible word. Most of us would rather not think of the importance of confession to our relationship with God and others. However, confession is primary to this. Being afraid and angry are not sins but can turn into them if we refuse to confess that they are real and are willing to do what is necessary to control them. It is a personal choice.

Today, most people would rather not use the word *confess.* Just blame circumstances or other people or whatever, rather than take an inner evaluation and accept the need for confession.

In reality, no matter how smug or arrogant a person may be, they are not self-sufficient. They deceive themselves. They may even be really good at covering up where they are in life. They may even wait until the dark-blue place has overtaken them before they admit they are in need.

To be a healthy person, it is essential to take ownership of life. Confession is another step in the process of overall health.

That day long ago, after I left the doctor's office, I stopped and placed my head on the steering wheel of my little jeep and wept. I confessed I had become consumed by confusion and, yes, even doubt. I confessed I had lost my focus and perspective and that I could not handle this alone, and that I needed God to empower me with His Word and His knowledge if I were to experience victory over the dark blue. Even though the situation was different this time, I confessed that I must face cancer in this same way.

Are confusion, anger, doubt, or fear sins that should be confessed? No and yes. Emotions by themselves are not sin because we are by nature made up of various and sometimes conflicting feelings. However, ignoring potentially damaging emotions just leads to other complications.

I knew that my spiraling emotions were going to eventually damage me. It was difficult for me to face all these feelings but I knew I had to. You may need to consider this, too.

Wouldn't it be boring if we were like robots? The new AI (artificial intelligence) robots may be smart with data and facts but will never be capable of understanding the depth of emotions.

Accepting that we are made up of a myriad of emotions and then learning how to manage them is the secret.

Once it is determined that an emotion is more than a natural response but has become an embedded sin, then initiatives must be taken as to how to deal with this. Confession may be necessary. Negative emotions left unattended potentially can entwine the very core of the spirit. That is when they may become sin. Unconfessed sin inhibits God from drawing close and being active.

He will hold back His wisdom and blessing to anyone who continues to live with unconfessed sin.

Another question is, *Where are the emotions rooted?* For example an unwillingness to forgive may stem from some experience that occurred in years past. It is more difficult to forgive when the hurt inflicted wasn't warranted.

Whether you are an innocent party or guilty of the hurt, suppressing an unforgiving spirit will hold back the ability to move into a brighter-blue place in life.

Have you ever known anyone who refuses to forgive? Forgiveness is powerful. It brings to the forefront what may have been lurking and repressed in the dark place for a very long time.

Forgiveness may, in fact, be one sided. Expressing forgiveness does not require a response. It is personally liberating. An unforgiving spirit is sin so it requires a cleansing in the inner person before the bright blue can return.

Healing from within definitely will impact overall health. It especially affects attitudes and outlooks. My family can attest to this.

Repentance

Acceptance and confession are places to start but then there is repentance. What good was it going to do me to confess what I needed and then not repent of my weakness?

Repentance is the willingness to turn from where you are and stretch into the area of trust. That trust lies in a personal relationship with God and His Son, Jesus Christ. Exercising faith to trust in His wisdom and guidance and following through is repentance.

As I face the uncertainty of where cancer might lead me, I have to deal regularly with my weakness. I know what I must do. I have to ask for forgiveness for not trusting in Jesus' ability to walk with me. Sometimes I have to seek forgiveness and repentance daily. Spiritual cleanliness is essential to the bright blue only found in Jesus Christ.

Since I want to live in God's bright-blue beauty, I have to make personal choices. I have to ask God to deliver me. So, again, *What is repentance?* It is acknowledging the need for God and asking Him to give you His power. His Son, Jesus is the answer.

If you are struggling, are you willing to follow the steps to return to a brighter place of blue?

Receiving

Once I confessed my state of personal pity, repented of my inadequacies, and then asked for God's forgiveness, He opened my eyes to receive His love and care.

Repentance brought me back to Him; then He began to restructure my thoughts and return me to emotional health. I decided to receive His promises. They are true for all people for all time.

I had to choose. Would I allow Him to restore me? Every day, as I ask Him to keep me from sliding back into the dark blue place, He brightens me.

You may need to confess that you have not trusted God in every area of your life. Then please accept your weakness and ask God for help. Do not cling to some underlying dark place like anger, hurt, pain, rejection. Only you can name your dark blue place or places. Open up to God and He will open you up to a brighter-blue place.

---

1 John 1:9
"If we claim to be without sin, we deceive ourselves. The truth is not in us. If we confess our sins, He is faithful and just and will forgive us and cleanse us from all our unrighteousness."

Questions for you to consider:

1. Fear, anger, and anxiety in themselves are not sin but what we do with them might be. Is there a need for you to go through the steps to be restored to a brighter-blue place?
2. Are there unresolved areas in your life that prevent you from having a daily relationship with God?
3. Will you depend on God to fulfill all His promises to you?
4. Are you willing to start with Scripture to find the promises of God to help you? Put to memory the one most special to you.

19

Lessons Learned along the Path

Lesson 1—Listen

We are all on a journey that will end in eternity. As a Christian, I know the ultimate end of my life. Heaven awaits me. Most people do not consider the link between birth to their final destination. The eternal journey is set but there are different paths to choose along the journey. Can one choice make a difference? Answer: Yes! Making one choice can lead down a path we neither hoped for nor expected.

My cancer diagnosis shifted everything onto a different path. I certainly never thought I would have cancer. Who does?

Those words immediately caused me to face a new path in life. Along my journey, I clung to Jerry and our family. They have been gracious to walk with me. They make even the darkest of blue days a bit brighter.

When I had time to process the news of cancer, I began to ask questions: *Do I really believe God has a plan and what does this mean? Will I be cured? Am I going to face years of treatments, etc.? How long might I live? What cancer clinic should I go to? Can I trust God to lead me to the right medical team? What about Jerry and our family?* If you have faced cancer, I am sure you have asked similar questions and more.

Lesson 2—Pay Attention

When my head finally cleared and my emotions settled down, I asked God the ultimate question: "How can I be a Kingdom person for You, Lord, during this process, no matter what that might mean?"

I did not want to return to a self-absorbed, depressed place of dark blue. I decided I wanted to be an example of God's grace, His plan, and His provision. Yes! I made a personal choice.

I knew that God was leading me when I was nudged by His Holy Spirit to go for a mammogram. I tried to deny that I might need one. My General Physician did not suggest it, but there was a nagging nudge I couldn't ignore.

I went for the mammo; then a biopsy was scheduled. The result, on December 16, 2021, was cancer in the left breast.

Our daughter in love, Lisa, is an oncology nurse. We talked over the biopsy results and she suggested I go to the Baptist Cancer Center in Memphis to the Breast Unit. I will be forever grateful for her counsel.

I called on December 17 and was scheduled for an appointment for another more in-depth biopsy on December 20. The results of that test confirmed a cancerous node on the interior of the left breast. Very small. Non-invasive. No margins or lymph glands affected. Phase I—Triple Positive. I then met with the surgeon and oncologist to discuss treatment options.

A zoom call was scheduled between the doctors to discuss my particular case. They were in agreement as to my diagnosis. I liked the personal care I received. I knew I was not simply another patient but that I would receive the best care from this medical team.

The plan was clear: chemo, surgery, radiation, and extended treatment. That set the new path. I began treatment on January 14, 2022.

Before I agreed to the treatment plan, I called several people who had experience with breast cancer to seek their perspective. I quickly learned that each experience is unique. For some women, getting a second opinion is good. Your choice as to your medical treatment will impact the overall picture of your future. You need as much information as possible.

Doctors can misdiagnose, so do not be intimidated when a doctor seems to be offended when you say you want to get another opinion. With cancer, a second opinion may bring clarity as to what your next steps will be. A misdiagnosis may result in the spread of the disease with it metastasizing into other areas. Quick action is needed.

In Memphis, I met the most amazing team of care givers. The doctors, nurses, and assistants all work together with one goal: serving the patient—in this case, me.

The prognosis given to me from the beginning is very positive. With treatment and follow up, I should live many more years.

Lesson 3—Be Alert

My first day in chemotherapy was daunting. I had never been in a chemo lab before and certainly did not know what to expect. I prayed that morning that God would show me what He had planned. During my quiet time, my thoughts took me back to the Bible story of Job. He faced the ultimate test. In chapters 1 and 2, we see Job's desperate situation. Everything was taken away from him. He did not waver in his trust in God in spite of family and friends who tried to analyze why God was allowing this to happen to him.

Job's responses are valuable. Only God can give peace, comfort, and direction when we have a crisis. Satan tried to shatter Job. Job was shaken and stirred but not shattered.

Another thing I learned from Job was that Satan had to ask permission from God in order to try to take Job down. God granted the request and the story of Job began. Job was blessed in the end of his story more than in the beginning. You can read his story for yourself.

I knew that God was testing me just like He did Job. How would I respond to this test? Would I buckle under? How would my body react to treatment? Would I allow this experience to take me into a dark blue place of doubt and despair? *God, will You show me a purpose in all of this?*

How do you respond to unexpected situations?

Lesson 4—Engage

I made a choice to trust God no matter what the test might be. I decided I would not allow this to shatter me. The days might be a bit darker blue, but I was going to refuse to return to the deep-blue place I had been in before.

As I entered the chemo lab, I asked the nurse where I should sit. She said, "Why don't you go sit next to her?" I took a seat and noticed the lady to my right. I simply said to her, "Those shoes are cute." We began a conversation about her cancer experience. I knew immediately that God was going to let me see His display of power in that dreary, foreboding place. This lady became Number 1 in the group I now call my "chemo friends."

I also noticed another, much-younger lady to her right who was not engaging with anyone except her nurse. Her face was down into her cell phone. Cell phones are a great place to escape. As she was leaving, I heard the nurse offer her a "Happy Birthday." I placed a check in my mind to think about this later.

God led me to prepare a small birthday bag for her. It was nothing special. Just a note pad, pen, bookmark, and a belated "Happy Birthday" wish.

I placed it on her chemo table the next week. She didn't open it right away, but then the next week she motioned for me to sit by her. She became Number 2. I learned that she was thirty-one and had been diagnosed while nursing her baby daughter. We began a texting group as a way to encourage each other.

The two of us were joined the next week by Number 3. Each week, I waited in anticipation to see what new person the Lord would bring across my path. Number 3 said her cancer experience included several, family members, including two sisters. She said she had waited to go to the doctor. In waiting her cancer became more advanced. Her treatment will be more involved.

Please go for your regular mammogram tests. If I had waited longer, my cancer would have expanded. If I had gone earlier, it would not have been noticed. Just go regularly!

Then came Number 4. The three of us were busy trading "chemo chat" when I noticed a lady across from us. I asked her if this was her first time in the lab. She said she had found a lump. She and her husband were in the process of building a new home so she was talking about all the added stress from her diagnosis. Cancer never comes at a good time.

That started an interaction with the other three as they began to share back and forth. I just listened. From then on, our group of four sat close in the chemo chairs so we could talk. I think when there is open communication, a lot can be learned. We were there the same day each week.

Treatment usually lasts about two hours, which gives plenty of time to listen and learn. The girls teased me because some of the meds would not make me sleepy when it caused them to nod off. Talking together makes the time pass faster.

Then came Number 5. That day, we were settling into our chemo chairs when I noticed a lady directly across from me. Again, I simply said, "I like your hat." She responded. Then I asked, "Is this your first time in chemo?"

She said, "Yes, and I am terrified." I could see the fear and uncertainty on her face. Immediately the other four jumped in to encourage her with what to expect and not to be afraid. Each week, I was more overwhelmed with what God was doing.

Over the next twelve weeks, as we developed our growing texting group, I watched and read their words of support for each other. They offered not only encouragement, but mounds of valuable information.

If you are on a cancer path, find a small group of others whom you can link with. You might find this a wonderful source of strength, courage, and comfort. There are many large cancer support groups, but I think there is value in a small group where you can get to know each other on a more personal level.

Then came Number 6., a young single lady—scared and uncertain. I engaged her casually, but then she began a deeper conversation. I asked her if she would like to be part of our texting group. By this time, some of the girls had moved to another level of treatment and were not at the lab each week, so the texting group became the primary source of connection.

Number 7, like me, was the oldest. She did not want to be part of the large group but we have stayed in contact several times each week. She encourages me. Being the same age and basically with the same diagnosis, we relate in the same way.

I have grown to know the nursing staff pretty well over the weeks of treatment. Most of the nurses have been working in oncology for a long time and I know why: they love their work! I have watched them care for each patient in beautiful, loving, and caring ways. We certainly need that.

On another morning, as I entered the lab, I asked my nurse where I should sit. She said, "Anywhere is fine." Then she stopped and said, "Could you sit by the lady in the corner? This is her first time."

I took my seat and nodded toward her and her husband. I said, " I haven't noticed you here before. Is this your first time?"

She responded with, "Yes, and I'm scared."

I introduced myself and learned that it was their twentieth wedding anniversary, interrupted by cancer. She became Number 8. There are now twenty-four ladies in two groups of "Chemo Friends." One is a younger group and the other group is more like me, a bit older. Going through the process isn't ever easy but having a group like this makes me anticipate each new week of treatment.

As we shared, I heard the anxiety in Number 8's voice as she worried about to what to expect. I asked her if she wanted to be part of our texting group. She joined. Again, it has been amazing to watch how God works to accomplish His plan. His peace can overshadow any dark blue place.

Fear is an amazing thing. You can see it in the eyes and read it in the body language. I know that was one of the first emotions I experienced, too.

God has taught me that even a *simple servant* like me, who is willing to seek Him even in the most challenging situations of life, will be used for His glory and for a Kingdom purpose. Try it and you will see.

I believe you will only find what you need when you seek a deep personal relationship with God through Jesus. You will need to lean heavily on Him, more than ever before. You will need to push aside all pride, vanity, and self-assurance and admit to weakness, fear, and maybe even anger. He is stronger than any emotion and He offers His strength, courage, comfort, and healing.

You may not be healed of cancer, your marriage may be gone, you may have children that you know will never be retrieved from a world of addiction, or your spouse may have died and your life changes. The assurance you *can* have is to know that God cares. He loves you as though you were His only child. Hard to understand, isn't it? But the truth of Scripture will reside in you to bring you comfort because of God's love and compassion.

Our God is merciful and gracious. He inhabits the praise of His children. He wants you to seek Him. He is available through His Word. He will dwell in any heart that is open to His healing and will bring back from the darkest place of blue the one who seeks His truth, comfort, and restoration. He is the place of bright blue.

The more you seek God and rest in His ultimate plan and purpose, you will find exactly what you need to meet the deepest needs of your life.

Although professional help is sometimes needed and good counselors can guide and redirect their clients back from despair, I believe that only in Jesus and His power given by His Holy Spirit can any person return to the bright-blue place of His peace.

You will not find inner peace, joy, and spiritual rest anywhere but in Jesus.

John 14:27

"My peace I leave with you; my peace I give to you, not as the world gives. Let not your heart be troubled, neither let it be afraid."

Peace is a gift given to those who choose to believe in Jesus Christ as Savior. He also bestows on every one of His children the gift of the Holy Spirit. He is our guide into all truth and gives us the ability to discern between what is of God and what is not.

He establishes in us the strength, courage, and the character of Christ if we will only submit and obey. In Christ, there are no negatives. No dark-blue places can reside in the bright-blue light of Jesus.

Questions for you to consider:

1. Will you trust Jesus and depend on Him to bring you peace?
2. Will you seek Scripture from the Bible that will reassure you of the power available to help you navigate life's circumstances?

20

Where to Find What You Need

---

s I asked people to share about their life challenges, I was astounded. There were so many different situations, but it became clear that God has a simple plan. When followed, this plan will enable any person to return to a brighter-blue place from even the deepest pits of despair or depression.

We tend to make life much more difficult than is necessary. It takes simple faith to believe and trust that God really and truly does have the answers when there seems to be none.

The Bible is our guide book. It is all truth. It is the standard that God has given us to help us make sense of our crazy, unpredictable lives. It is clear on every level. It is so clear that even a small child can understand what we as adults often make overly complicated.

When I first experienced depression, I knew where to find solace and answers. God took me to His Word. I didn't want to go there. I was rebelling with all my questions and anger. But once I had reached the lowest point on the path of feeling lost and useless, and again on the path of cancer, I went searching in my Bible for comfort. Why the Bible?

I knew I would find what I needed in its pages. God speaks through His Word. Doesn't it seem almost too easy to think that, in the Bible, all the issues of life are addressed? But they are. You might consider this as an option when you reach your lowest point, too.

This last portion of my book will look deeply at one of the clearest pictures of depression in all of the Bible. There are many examples of people who struggled with their emotions but one stood out for me.

Hannah, the mother of Samuel, was my inspiration.

21

The Story of Hannah

As a child, I loved the story of Samuel but had never taken a close analytical look at Hannah, his mother. God carried me right back to that particular place in His Word to uncover for me the steps necessary to move any person out of the darkest-blue challenge or crisis back to a brighter-blue place in life.

---

1 Samuel 2:2

"There is no one Holy like the Lord. There is no one besides you; there is no Rock like our God."

The Story of Hannah

Did you know you have a background story? We all have one. How did you become the person you are today? What are some of the experiences that have had an impact on you? Your return to the bright side of blue from the dark-blue place may take you back in your past. Mine did.

God took me back to my childhood and the Bible class at church. On the wall hung large pictures of many Bible stories. My favorite was the story of Samuel. I knew the story but had never really looked deeply at the other parts to his story—until recently.

As I began to explore the life of Samuel, I recalled the picture of Samuel leaning in closely to Eli to hear what God was saying through that old man. I said to God, "Since You have made me recall the story of Samuel, what do You want me to learn from this?" I picked up my Bible and began to read 1 Samuel, and the story of Hannah.

Hannah, the mother of Samuel, has been used throughout the ages as an example of a woman of faith and prayer. Bible classes and prayer groups have been named after her. Mary, our Lord's mother, used the prayer of Hannah as a model for her own prayer in Luke 2. Little girls are named Hannah in respect of this incredible lady. However, her story begins in a dark-blue place.

Who was she? What was her background story? Why is this important to the life of Samuel and who he would become? Does God really use the background stories of our lives?

As the life of Hannah unfolds, we see how God was preparing her for the future. Hannah's story was crucial to the birth and development of Samuel and the shaping of his character and attributes.

I found in Hannah a perfect example of a woman who was overwhelmed. She was stressed, frustrated, oppressed, and confused. She had moved into the dark-blue place of hopelessness.

This wasn't just a blue day, it was a dark-blue life. She went from discouragement to despondency, despondency to despair, and despair to depression—a spiral. The problems were in every area of her life: cultural, marital, religious, physical, emotional, social, relational, and spiritual. The pit of depression was deep.

I was enthralled by the story. Hanna was overwhelmed. Her relationships were sour. Her attitude was stinky. Her health was broken and she was emotionally unstable. She was in a dark-blue place.

An intimate look into her life reveals a perfect, step-by-step example of how to have victory no matter how dark blue the place may be.

There is hope. God cares. He intervened for Hannah and can for you, too.

What might have happened if Hannah had not overcome her depression? What if she hadn't chosen to lay herself bare before God? You might say, "Well, God would have raised up someone else." Yes. True, but look at what would have been lost to Hannah and her family. Moreover, look at what would have been lost to you and me!

From Genesis all the way through the Bible, we see how God intervenes in lives. Both in the Old and New Testaments there are stories of people who were in dark-blue places in life. It might be good for you to explore some of these poignant stories to see where their lives took a turn from bright blue to the dark-blue place and what was the ultimate outcome. What did the Bible characters discover about God and themselves, and how to become victorious and be restored to a bright-blue place in which to dwell?

I have the most frightening and overwhelming health issue of our day, cancer. It isn't a journey I chose to walk, but God has placed it here for His purpose. What will I discover along this path?

Although Hannah did not have cancer, she did have multiple issues that could have inhibited her from becoming all that God had planned. Hannah was in a dark-blue place.

Can cancer be a bright-blue place or will it become a dark place of fear and dread?

> ### Psalm 139:16
> *"Your eyes saw my unformed body. All the days ordained for me were written in your Book before one of them came to be."*

Depression has talons that may wrap around the emotions and cause instability in every area of life. As is true for all of us in these situations, she had to address some personal and vital issues.

Questions for you to consider:

1. What do you know of your background story?
2. Do you know how your name was chosen?
3. Do you know the meaning of your name?
4. How have the events of your life influenced you?
5. Do you believe God has a plan for your life?

22

The Spiral Begins

1. Connected by Birth

1 Samuel 1: 1—"There was a man …"

The ancestry of Elkanah and Hannah is significant to the life of Samuel. We know nothing about Hannah's history as she is not mentioned until 1 Samuel 1. We do know that God knew her heart. She was given a special honor and place in the history of Israel.

Elkanah was a descendent of the tribe of Levi as seen in Exodus 6 and 1 Chronicles 6. God gave this tribe special duties which enabled them to be involved in tabernacle worship. This connection allowed Samuel to be placed as an assistant to Eli, the high priest.

2. Captured by Culture

1 Samuel 1:2—"He had two wives …"

It was allowed and customary in that day for men to have more than one wife. My husband says this is ridiculous. "One wife is enough for any man."

Having multiple wives may have been accepted but it was a huge problem. Hannah had to share her husband with another wife, Peninnah. This was the beginning of Hannah's spiral into the dark-blue place.

In the fifties and sixties in America, the nuclear family of two parents who had never been divorced was common. Divorce was rare. The culture revolved around community, church, jobs, school, and activities. Most parents knew what their children were involved in and who their friends were. The doors at home were not locked and we were not afraid to play anywhere in the neighborhood. Little by little that changed.

Television programming was mostly clean and family oriented. One cultural trend that I think influenced homes was the introduction of soap operas. This brought infidelity, deceit, and disgrace into our homes. I remember once asking my mother why she watched the soaps. Her reply was, "They are so true to life." My thought then and now was, *It's not true in our home.*

National conflict moved into our living rooms. We watched global war and violence increase. Riots and hatred have filtered into our homes.

The influences of culture play a major role in how we form our beliefs and the effect this has on our standards of living and on our homes. The home you grow up in, where you grew up, your friends, the school you attend, etc., all contribute to the person you will become. The results of changing cultural trends will shift how the family processes those trends and how their influence can change the family. The shift may be so slow that few even take notice. Elkanah was living in a situation that was culturally and legally accepted, but his family was a wreck.

A healthy home is not a perfect home, but should be where love abounds and family members are encouraged to reach their full potential. The present culture of America has changed the landscape of society and particularly the home. The very nature of the family is being challenged. Husbands are often demeaned as weak and less important than the wife. Family issues and parenting are no longer shared in the home but are governed by "societal" correctness. Children have become the focus of family life and activities. Sports are paramount and social media and the internet have become the way to communicate, even at home.

The changing perception of commitment has brought confusion into thousands of relationships. Education is being used to promote liberal ideologies. Teachers are being instructed and trained in ways to alter how children think about history, literature, science, and themselves. Gender confusion is rampant.

The biblical worldview, upholding basic standards set by God, are no longer held as the plumbline of education. School and college are now the seedbed for the undermining of our entire society.

Consider how the relaxed attitudes regarding sexuality (premarital, marital and homosexual) are changing family life. Homosexual and transgender issues are the focus of many advertisements and debates. Surgeries to alter the sex of even the youngest of children are being touted as acceptable. Parents are being intimidated by "professionals" to promote the changing of the sex of their children.

Television programs are designed and written to push the reducing of the husband and father to a subordinate role in the home and to promote the elimination of the traditional family unit. This standard was set by God and is the basis of all societies. When this is gone, our entire culture will quickly collapse.

Indecency in both speech and dress aggravate this issue. Ideas contrary to wholesome values of morality and decency are continually pushed. Addictions such as pornography and drugs of every sort threaten and destroy. Pornography may begin with an innocent exposure to an image or an accidental web search. Curiosity may be the enticement which leads to the deep, dark-blue world of sexual perversion.

The casual use of alcohol as a social norm may lead to alcoholism. Pain that becomes intolerable may lead to an addition to pain medication. Overuse, then abuse, can lead to a life of addiction. Addiction may begin with a genetic connection. Systemic addiction may then run through families for several generations. Gambling has become a legal and accepted form of entertainment.

More pressure than ever is on every area of life to compromise and adapt to societal change.

Cultural shifts have also invaded the church. Many pastors no longer preach, "Thus says the Lord." Many have compromised the gospel. The "feel-good" worship has often replaced biblical messages. This approach will result in the questioning of Scripture. The redefining of terms such as family, marriage, commitment, religion, behavior, respect, and love has invaded our churches.

On a larger scale, consider how cultural trends have pervaded our nation and world. No longer are the standards of God held as the guideposts for life. Cultural norms must be weighed carefully for their value. Any time we embrace the cultural trends of a godless society, it will cause major havoc on homes and families. Trends continue to spiral downward, away from the traditional family and Christian values. This shift may be subtle but destructive.

To deny the impact of cultural change on families and society is ignorance. The tide has turned and what was once a bright-blue place in our society has become a dark-blue place.

For Elkanah, Hannah, and Penninah the accepting of cultural trends and views on family life penetrated into the core of their home. It is clear to see how this shift captivated and almost destroyed Hannah and impacted their family.

The influence of culture is the first pressure point that contributed to Hannah's slide into a dark-blue place. How a family deals with changing culture will impact marriage and home life.

> ### Exodus 14:11
> "They said to Moses, 'What have you done to us by bringing us out of Egypt? It would have been better for us to serve the Egyptians than to die in the wilderness!'"

Elkanah and Hannah were captured by the culture of the day. Be wary about cultural shifts.

Questions for you to consider:

1. How easy is it to become satisfied within the culture rather than face conflict?
2. Read 1 Samuel chapter 1 in your Bible. What influence did Elkanah have on his wives? What reaction did both Hannah and Peninnah have to Elkanah? Was this a cultural shift from what God initially intended for the family? How?
3. Do you let the events of your life influence you for the positive or negative?
4. Has cultural change impacted your family?
5. Where might current cultural shifts lead our nation? Are we on a slippery slope to the dissolution of the family?

23

Marriage Madness

1 Samuel 1:2

"One was called Hannah. The other one was named Peninnah."

Another point of contention for this family was that Hannah had no children. It was assumed that a wife would have a child. Not only did Peninnah have one, but she had several.

Hannah was forced to share the affection and commitment of her husband, Elkanah, with his "other" wife, Peninnah. Even though this was an accepted practice, both women had a problem with the situation.

Think about this family and their lives. Form a picture. Perhaps in one tent you have Peninnah and her children and in the tent next door you have Hannah.

As a husband, where might Elkanah rather spend his time? With a brooding wife in one tent or at least with the laughter and innocence of children in the other?

Poor Elkanah. How sad that he had to try to satisfy two unhappy women. It must have been difficult for him to stay positive in spite of the stress. Could this have led Elkanah into a dark-blue place? He must have felt like a juggler. How would you like to try to be a peacemaker in the middle of that chaos?

Many families live in chaos today. Priorities are out of order. Dads and moms are trying to juggle work, their kids' activities, and other responsibilities. Add to this stress the threat of violence pervading every area, including creating unsafe school environments. Each day we hear of violence and death. Cities have become a war zone. Often going to church together has moved to the bottom of the priority list.

We have found, in spite of all the negative publicity the religious community has received, church is still the place to go for healthy relationships. (That being said, a warning here to parents: no matter whether it is getting to know your children's teacher, a coach, your children's friends, neighborhood activity, or church program, all parents must be in touch with everything to which their family is exposed. You can no longer assume that your children are safe and their minds protected. They are vulnerable and impressionable.)

Children may be easily influenced to accept any blowing wind of loud voices. Make sure your home is where the standards of God and His clear voice are proclaimed. Establish your home on His Word and then live out by faith His standards. Elkanah was challenged with the blowing winds of discord yet he was strong.

Genesis 12:7

"The Lord appeared to Abraham and said, 'To you and your off-springs I will give this land.'"

Throughout the Bible, we see examples of both healthy and unhealthy families. Abram remains throughout the ages as an illustration of one who sought God as the spiritual leader of his family. It wasn't a perfect family. Read his story in your Bible, beginning in Genesis 12.

Questions for you to consider:

1. From one to ten with ten being the ideal, how would you rate the climate in your home?
2. Would you say your family is in need of a "spiritual tune up"?
3. Would you say your family emphasizes the importance of God in your home?
4. What is required for a family to have a brighter-blue family life?

24

Worship Worries

1 Samuel 1:3
"Year by year this man went up from his town to worship and sacrifice in Shiloh to the Lord Almighty."

When Elkanah sacrificed, he would give portions to Peninnah his wife and to all her sons and her daughters but to Hannah he would give a double portion for he loved Hannah, but the Lord had closed her womb. Elkanah was not only dedicated to God, but he was also consistent in his worship. Each year he would faithfully take his family up to the tabernacle.

Sometime there is conflict in the home over where to go to church or even if church will be part of the life of the family. Our pastor in Florida, Dr. Homer G. Lindsay, Jr., would often say, "The husband should be the spiritual head of the home." Jerry has preached for years that if the husband will take the lead in praying over his family and read even a small portion of Scripture every day with his family, it will have eternal results. It will also reap a bountiful return throughout the years of family living. I have personally seen how God honors a godly husband and father.

Jerry began this practice from the start of our marriage. He continued even as he traveled in full-time evangelism. If he was anywhere in the continental United States, he would call home every morning at 7:00 our time. He would read a scripture and have a short prayer with Drew and Becca. That's dedication and commitment.

Elkanah made sure he was being an example of faithfulness to his family. A point worth mentioning is the atmosphere in the place of worship. It states that the priestly sons of Eli, Hophni and Phinehas, were there. Why is this important? You can discover the details of these bad boys in 1 Samuel 2. The point is: not all religious people are reliable. Religion is not the answer to returning from the dark-blue place.

Another point is that not all members of the family have an attitude of worship. Although Elkanah was faithful and obedient and gave a portion to Peninnah and a double portion to Hannah, it didn't cure the issues that were swirling around these two women. Do you think Peninnah knew that Elkanah was giving Hannah a double portion to sacrifice and only giving her "a portion"? That might cause a disturbance.

Elkanah's love for Hannah is apparent and Peninnah must have sensed this. It labels Peninnah as a "rival" to Hannah who provoked her bitterly to irritate her. Might this contribute to Hannah's spiraling into the dark-blue place?

I've often said, "There's nothing meaner than a mean-spirited woman." They plot, scheme, and make people's lives miserable. This describes Peninnah.

This was not a short -erm problem for Hannah; this went on regularly. The apex was annually when they would all go "up to worship." The meanness, provoking, badgering, and constant ridicule was out in the open. Can't you sense the despair that Hannah must have been feeling? Emotions are real and certainly can be the key to a spiraling into the dark-blue places of life.

It appears that Hannah thought her despondency was a result of her being childless. She grieved over not having children.

When we examine the situation a bit more closely, doesn't it seem that, in God's providential wisdom, perhaps He closed Hannah's womb because she was not yet spiritually prepared to be the mother Samuel would need to prepare him for God's service as a man?

Think about it. How many mothers have been instrumental, too, in raising children to become successful? How many athletes, when interviewed, will give thanks to their mothers for the influence they had on their lives? It is difficult to raise children in our world today, but for Hannah, it was the key to Samuel's future.

God knew that Samuel would need a very special mother to prepare him for what was to come. His father was also instrumental. What about your children? How are you preparing them for their future?

> **Jeremiah 1:5**
> *"Before I formed you in the womb, I knew you. Before you were born I set you apart. I appointed you as a prophet to the nations."*

Consider what God might have planned for your children. The Bible reveals how God prepared His servants even from the womb. Each baby is a special gift. Many babies are conceived in unusual circumstances but, regardless, God has a plan for each child.

Questions for you to consider:

1. What do you believe about the unborn child and why do you believe the way you do?
2. What would have been the outcome if Hannah had never had Samuel? Also consider if Mary had taken a drastic measure when she learned she was going to become pregnant as an unwed mother.
3. Read John 15:11–32 in your Bible, Jesus' parable of "the prodigal son." Your child may be wayward like the prodigal son, but look at the hope that the prodigal's father had in God.

25

A Sensitive Spouse

> **1 Samuel 1:8**
> "Elkanah, her husband, would say to her, 'Hannah, why do you weep, not eat and why is your heart sad? Am I not better to you than ten sons?'"

Poor Elkanah. He knew Hannah wasn't eating. He saw the downcast expression on her face. He tried to express empathy and compassion to Hannah. What a man! He knew that Hannah really wanted children. He knew there was a problem between his two wives. He tried to console Hannah as best he could. All his attempts had failed. She was spiraling further with each passing year. She was desperate. She must have thought, *No hope for me.*

Can you appreciate the sensitivity of Elkanah?

Jerry has stood by me through my cancer experience. He has cooked, cleaned, protected me, and consoled me when I was moving into a dark place emotionally. Offered a shoulder to lean on. A good man is a treasure. There are some things that even a good man cannot fix. When even the best spouse has no answer to the issues, God does!

One verse that I hold close is: Proverbs 14:1. *"The wise woman builds her house but the foolish one tears hers down with her own hands."*

My blue days often wear on Jerry and my family. I have to take responsibility for the way my emotions impact them. I have met many women who will not take responsibility for what is going on in their homes. They will not acknowledge their part in creating the home environment.

Whether we accept this or not, God ordained marriage, home, and family. The husband is the head. The wife the helpmate. The wife has certain responsibilities, as does the husband.

Do you not believe that, as God established the home, He created two individuals who would come together to form the unit? Yes, we are two individuals with two distinct personalities. We have strengths and weaknesses but, when brought together, this becomes the foundation on which God can create the beauty of marriage. It is when we reject our place in the plan of God that we get into trouble. A wife can destroy her marriage.

Marriages have been built and broken on Ephesians 5: 22–32.

Husbands who lord over their wives and wives who continue to usurp the role of their husband are both doing damage to what God planned. God says that just as Christ loved the church and gave His life for it, so a husband ought to love his wife. The wife, in turn, should be able to trust and have respect in her husband as the head of the home. Love, respect, trust, and commitment are the basics. We either accept these or see the results of our decisions when we reject God's ultimate plan.

In the home of Elkanah, Hannah had lost her ability to trust her husband. She had become focused on what she did not have, what Peninnah did have, and what Elkanah could not provide.

Often when one spouse begins to shift his or her focus away from the commitment that was once so special onto other areas or people, things begin to fall apart. What may have been a bright-blue marriage at the start becomes a midnight-blue place where no brightness resides.

Children often are caught up in split allegiances. Friends may offer advice that is rejected. It may seem like all hope is lost. Hannah was in that place.

Recently I learned of a marriage that could not survive the shock and uncertainty of a cancer diagnosis. When they needed each other in one of the most desperate times, they decided to call their marriage quits. Were there other underlying problems? Probably. However, no place is so dark or desperate that God cannot intervene—and miracles do happen.

Never underestimate what God can and will do when we are willing to allow Him to make the changes that might be necessary to restore relationships to a bright-blue place.

What will it take to restore a home to a bright-blue place from the dark-blue place?

Malachi 2:16

" 'I hate divorce, says the Lord God of Israel.'"

God's standard for marriage is clear. He ordained the union between man and woman as the model for marriage for all society. God hates divorce but He loves the divorced person. How do you counsel someone who has been divorced and remarried?

We have many friends in this situation. God alone has omniscient wisdom. He counsels and guides. We see from a human observation point. God looks at every aspect of every situation from His point of view.

Questions for you to consider:

1. If you are married to the same spouse for many years, how do you view divorce? Do you have an attitude of superiority toward others?
2. If you are divorced and remarried, did you and your spouse ask God for His guidance?
3. Should Elkanah have considered divorcing Peninnah?

26

Blue Brightens

---

1 Samuel 1:10
"Then she, greatly distressed, prayed to the Lord and wept bitterly."

Have you ever been so desperate that you did not know what to do? Hannah was there. Health failing. Marriage in shambles. Peninnah mean and hateful. Elkanah kind and good. A dark-blue place.

What does it take to reverse the dark-blue place? For me, a diagnosis of cancer will never be erased. Yes, there is treatment, a great prognosis, but the nagging word "cancer" still lingers. When that word comes into my thoughts, I shove it aside. I claim it under the promise that God will guide me through and that ultimately healing rests in Him.

Am I a perfect person? Absolutely not, but I have a perfect God, a redeeming Savior, and the residence of the Holy Spirit. As we learn to rely on everything that God provides, He will restore!

Hannah, in her distress, prayed.

She wept. She made a decision. She vowed to the Lord. "If you will look on the affliction of your maidservant, and remember me, and not forget Thy maidservant, but will give Thy maidservant a son, then I will give him to the Lord all the days of his life and a razor will not touch his head" (1 Samuel 1:11).

When Hannah used the term "maidservant" she was placing herself under the full authority of God. His holiness, His authority, His wisdom and His plan. She then added to her vow by promising that if God would grant her a son, she would dedicate him to special service. A Nazarite was one who was consecrated for service to the Lord. She was not only willing to raise a son in a godly way, but also to instill in him that God had a special plan for his future.

As Hannah prayed, Eli the high priest was observing her. He saw her mouth moving, but there was no sound. Actually, he was mis-observing her. He thought she was drunk. Even someone who wants to be helpful can make the wrong observations and assumptions. He did.

She reassured him that she was, in fact not drunk. Then she made a monumental statement. She said, "I have *poured* out my soul before the Lord" (1 Samuel 1:15).

When we get serious with the Lord, He responds. Hannah reached into the depths of her heart and pulled out everything that she had been carrying for years. What? Perhaps anger, frustration, guilt, embarrassment, resentment, jealously, envy, hurt. You name it. She knew.

Only when she was willing to empty herself of everything that was holding onto her, and lay it all out before the Lord, was she restored. The dark-blue talons of discouragement and hopelessness began to fade away.

Don't you think it is much easier to shift negative emotions onto another person or thing than to have to address them personally? I do. How often have I had to call myself back to self-evaluation so I could better see things more clearly? The interesting thing about how God deals with people is He does so on an individual basis. My family is impacted by my attitudes, emotions, and actions. Hannah's was, too.

Her situation was not a recent one. She had been dealing with this for many years. It is true that the longer we push things aside, the more things pile up. Hannah's resentment and envy had grown into bitterness of spirit.

The fact is, the more we suppress negative emotions, the more likely it is that they will grow and morph into something even more ugly. She may have begun by dealing with her emotions privately but at this point they had become overt and apparent.

Scripture says Hannah wept and had stopped eating. She was sinking deeper into a dark-blue place. Everybody knew. Elkanah spoke to this and Peninnah continued to provoke her to make her even more miserable. This was a truly sad situation.

Only Hannah could deal with this. Bitterness is interesting. It grows and takes root. It is like a broad-leaf weed that must be dug up. You can't get rid of these simply by snipping off the top. You must dig down to the root area and then trowel it out. Hannah finally had the strength and courage to deal with the bitterness and root it out. Any time we allow bitterness to grow, it will take us into a deep, dark-blue place.

The "pouring process" is painful but totally liberating. The turning point for Hannah is found in 1 Samuel 1:9 which says, "Hannah stood up!"

Hannah had been cowering for years. She had been overwhelmed by the mean-spiritedness of Peninnah. In contrast, she had a compassionate husband. She may have felt guilty and embarrassed. Her pouring out process began as she stood up to face everything that had been nagging her.

The picture of Hannah weeping is a great picture of confession and repentance.

Are tears always a part of repentance? No. But her tears were cleansing away all that had consumed Hannah for years.

It isn't necessarily the tears that produce cleansing, but in her case it was an outward picture of the inward cleansing. It was visible. Eli took note.

Hannah prayed and offered a vow. A vow is taken seriously by God. Numbers 30:2 says, *"If a person makes a vow to the Lord or swears an oath to bind himself by some agreement, that word shall not be broken. They shall do according to all that proceeds out of their mouth."*

As Hannah prayed and Eli observed, he thought she must have been drunk. He probably had seen this before. He may have thought she wasn't serious again. Hannah spoke with authority and conviction as she assured Eli that she was indeed serious.

How often have I prayed in anguish?

How about you?

Eli simply affirmed that she was being heard by God.

---

1 Samuel 1:17
"Eli answered: 'Go in peace and may the God of Israel grant your petition that you have asked of Him.'"

Did Eli know that by the next year Hannah would have a baby boy? Did she leave her prayer time confident she would have a baby or did she simply place herself under the providential plan of God?

Either way, she knew that God had heard!

When you pray, do you know that God is listening? How do you approach God? Hannah first acknowledged God's place. Then she laid herself bare, all the way from her head to her toes.

Often in my personal prayer time I start by telling God what I want or need. He wants me to do this, but He loves to hear the praises of His children. Adoration, praise, worship, exaltation are where we should begin. Thanking God for His goodness. Being grateful for all that Jesus did and is doing. Also showing gratitude for the residence of the Holy Spirit and all that He provides.

Hannah started with adoration. In 1 Samuel 1:11, Hannah states: *"Oh Lord God of hosts." God inhabits the praise of His people."* Prayer is our link to the throne of God. Jesus always prayed asking for the will of the Father to be accomplished in Him. In the Garden of Gethsemane, we see Jesus in a most dark-blue place (Luke 22:39–46). There, He poured out His heart to the Father.

> ### Luke 22:44
> *"And being in anguish He prayed more earnestly and His sweat was like drops of blood falling to the ground."*

He was in deep distress. He knew what was facing Him and the outcome, yet He prayed in agony. He showed by example the pouring process. Jesus faced the abuse and ultimate death of the cross and He poured out to the Father His deepest emotions.

Questions for you to consider:

1. Do you know that, as a believer in Jesus, you have the Holy Spirit in you?
2. Do you know how to access the power, strength, courage, and reassurance of God through His Spirit?
3. Are you willing, as Hannah and Jesus did, to pour out your deepest emotions and needs to your heavenly Father?

27

Bright Blue Returns

> 1 Samuel 1:18
> "Let your maidservant find favor in your sight. So the woman went her way and ate and her face was no longer sad."

Hannah found the key to restoration: her willingness to lay herself bare, pour out her heart in prayer, acknowledge the power of God and then, the final piece of the picture, her willingness to "rest" in the Lord. The result for Hannah was immediate.

Often moving from a bright-blue place in life into the dark-blue valley doesn't happen overnight. It may be a slow process as the situations of life continue to pile up, forming a heaping mound of debris.

Yet, when we can accept the promises of God, the results are immediate. The Bible teaches that God's ear is always turned our way. He hears. He cares. He answers. His Holy Spirit resides in His child. His answers may not come in the way we are asking, but they will come. He will give peace, strength, courage, and "rest."

Hannah may or may not have known in her heart that God would grant her a baby. As she allowed God to restore her to a bright-blue place, she watched God's plan unfold. Are you willing to follow her example and rest in the Lord?

How do you know that God is listening, hearing, and caring? The first answer is simple. In the Word of God, it is clear that God is, indeed, listening to every word you say, every care you have, and every drama you may be living through or may face. And, there will be dramas and crises in life! Just call to Him! First John 5:14 tells us, *"This is the confidence we have in approaching God. If we ask anything according to His will, He hears us."*

The second answer to the question regarding if God listens is found in what Jesus said about the Holy Spirit in John 14:16, *"I will ask the Father and He will give you another Counselor to be with you forever, the Spirit of Truth."* The counsel of the Holy Spirit comes straight from the throne of God. He will serve you and restore you to the bright-blue place in life. He will guide you to self-search and then help you unwrap those dark talons that may have plagued you for years. Painful? Maybe. But remember: as we cleanse away the debris, there is Freedom! If you are willing to search the Bible for direction, you will find it.

The third answer to the question is in confirmation from outside. That may be from someone like Eli who simply offered a word of encouragement to Hannah. It may even come from some random encounter. An unexpected comment. Just pay attention and you will see how God listens, intervenes, and directs!

---

1 John 5:14
"This is the confidence we have in approaching God; that if we ask anything according to His will, He hears us."

Acknowledging that God is listening is the beginning place of restoration from the dark-blue places in life to the bright-blue of His grace.

As Hannah found her personal strength, she found she could ask God for what she considered the impossible. She may not have had immediate confirmation, but she was willing to rest in the fact that God heard her pleas and cries.

Questions for you to consider:

1. Have you ever trusted God for the impossible?
2. Do you seek answers from the Bible first, then from guidance from the Holy Spirit? Or do you go to a person first before asking God?

28

The Bright Side of Blue Continues

I began this book several years ago when I thought my life had ended. My nest had emptied out. I was getting older and facing physical changes and my emotions were spiraling out of control. *God, can You still use me? Lord, do You still have a plan?*

Personal examination led me to new adventures in ministry and service.

During the latest path on my life's journey, I have once again seen how God intervenes. The path changed. Cancer was daunting. Threatening. Uncertainty prevailed. Again, I asked God, *Are You through with me now?*

He answered. "I'm not finished with you."

He has revealed new avenues for me to see His power displayed. Being available to serve is all that is required. I asked. He again showed me a new part of His plan.

Over the past twenty-four months, I have become more aware than ever of God's presence, strength, power, and grace. I prayed. I poured. He heard. He is answering! Jerry and I have walked a stressful path, yet out of ashes has emerged beauty. We are committed to be God's servants.

Even a simple servant is of use when available. I am that simple servant.

For me, bright blue has returned.

My prayer is that wherever you are on the path of your life's journey, when it becomes dark-blue and gloomy, you know how to return to a brighter-blue place. This is a place where you can rest and grow. You can know that God has you in the very palm of His hand.

This confidence comes by trusting in Jesus, God's only Son. A personal relationship with Jesus ensures that His presence is within you in the form of the Holy Spirit. If you want to be restored no matter how dark blue your life may seem, just trust that Jesus can renew and rescue you!

Hannah did! I did! You can, too!

Steps to the Bright-Blue Place

1. **Acknowledge**
   Acknowledge where you are and how you came to be in that place.

2. **Accept**
   Accept that you are weak and cannot in yourself resolve the circumstance.

3. **Pray and pour out**
   Pray and pour out every care, woe, hurt and anxiety to the Lord.

4. **Make a commitment**
   A commitment means that you are willing to trust God completely in all areas.

5. **Rest**
   Lean heavily on your relationship with God. Stand firm on the strength and courage of Jesus. Ask the Holy Spirit to encircle you and He will provide you with wisdom for every step on your path.

6. **Worship**
   Go to worship, but be aware that worship isn't the place, music, sermon, or people. Worship begins as an attitude in the heart. Adoration, praise, and thanksgiving to God are elements of true worship.

Acknowledgments

Thank you, Jerry, my wonderful husband, for your continual encouragement and sometimes nagging to complete my book.

Thank you, son Drew and wife Lisa, and our daughter, Becca and her husband Josh, for your encouragement.

Thank you, Nick, Noah, Isa, Levi, and Hannah, our grandchildren. You continue to amaze me with your insights.

Thank you my new friend, Rhonda Barkley, for spending hours editing and making corrections to the text. Without God's intervention, I would not have met Rhonda and her husband, Paul.

Thank you to Arlyn Lawrence of Inspira Literary Solutions for her editorial expertise and ingenious ideas, and for formatting and refining the manuscript for publication.

Thank you to my publisher, Morgan James Publishing, for accepting the book, believing in its message, and bringing it to the world.

Thank you, Dr. Keith Williams, Dr. Sal Vasireddy, and Dr. Phillip Lammers who were with me when my journey began and throughout my continuing oncology treatments.

I thank the many people who were open and transparent in sharing with me their life stories.

I thank the Lord every day for allowing me to see His majesty, glory, and power. I see His handiwork everywhere, especially through the people I meet.

God has given me everything I need to walk me through this journey called "life." He shows me how to navigate the valleys and mountains along the way.

He has enabled me to move from cloudy, dark-blue days back into His bright-blue presence.

I thank God that He has given those of us who know Him personally the ability to view life from an eternal point of view and has given us instructions on how to cope with every situation we encounter.

Thank you from the bottom of my heart!

About the Author

Rebecca **(Becky) Drace** has been a Bible teacher in the US and internationally, alongside her husband of 54 years, Dr. Jerry Drace, specializing in family ministry and bringing hope and confidence to families and individuals around the world. Her daily devotion, "Becky the Bright Side" on Facebook delivers encouragement to many, as do the daily and weekly radio shows she and Jerry broadcast via American Family Radio. A team in marriage and ministry, Becky and Jerry have traveled the world and the airwaves sharing the good news of Jesus Christ.

Becky holds a BSW degree (Bachelor of Social Work) and a MSW (Master of Social Work) degree, which she completed at the age of fifty-nine. When asked why she went back to college during this season of life, she replied, "Jerry and our children encouraged me to reach a goal that I had not accomplished, and an extra level of credibility—even though I had practiced family ministry for many years. Also, it gives me the opportunity to encourage people who think they are too *old* to learn or too *old* to go back to college!"

Becky and Jerry have two grown, married children and five grandchildren. They make their home in Humboldt, Tennessee.

Becky may be reached through her website at www.hopeforthehome.org.

A free ebook edition is available with the purchase of this book.

To claim your free ebook edition:

1. Visit MorganJamesBOGO.com
2. Sign your name CLEARLY in the space
3. Complete the form and submit a photo of the entire copyright page
4. You or your friend can download the ebook to your preferred device

A **FREE** ebook edition is available for you or a friend with the purchase of this print book.

CLEARLY SIGN YOUR NAME ABOVE

Instructions to claim your free ebook edition:
1. Visit MorganJamesBOGO.com
2. Sign your name CLEARLY in the space above
3. Complete the form and submit a photo of this entire page
4. You or your friend can download the ebook to your preferred device

Print & Digital Together Forever.

Snap a photo

Free ebook

Read anywhere